24式太极拳习练与实战

主　编　於世海
副主编　朱小丽

吉林大学出版社
·长　春·

图书在版编目（CIP）数据

24式太极拳习练与实战 / 於世海主编 .— 长春：吉林大学出版社，2023.10

ISBN 978-7-5768-2441-4

Ⅰ .①2… Ⅱ .①於… Ⅲ .①太极拳—基本知识 Ⅳ .①G852.11

中国国家版本馆CIP数据核字（2023）第213577号

书　　名　24式太极拳习练与实战
　　　　　24SHI TAIJIQUAN XILIAN YU SHIZHAN

作　　者　於世海　主编
策划编辑　樊俊恒
责任编辑　刘　丹
责任校对　王宁宁
装帧设计　马静静
出版发行　吉林大学出版社
社　　址　长春市人民大街4059号
邮政编码　130021
发行电话　0431-89580028/29/21
网　　址　http://www.jlup.com.cn
电子邮箱　jldxcbs@sina.com
印　　刷　北京亚吉飞数码科技有限公司
开　　本　787mm × 1092mm　1/16
印　　张　12.75
字　　数　310千字
版　　次　2024年4月　第1版
印　　次　2024年4月　第1次
书　　号　ISBN 978-7-5768-2441-4
定　　价　78.00元

前　言

Preface

This textbook serves as a teaching tool for the simplified 24-Form Tai Chi, focusing on revealing the technical and practical aspects of each posture, and integrating the philosophical essence of Tai Chi culture throughout. Centered around students and guided by the principles of moral character cultivation, the aim is to foster students' love for and identification with Tai Chi and its cultural values. This university-level Tai Chi textbook adheres to standardized teaching methods, incorporating rich experiences from Tai Chi instruction and combat, while extending related theories and integrating the content of Tai Chi movements, techniques, breathing, and practical application into the textbook.

This textbook is a companion to the Chinese University MOOC and the national first-class course titled "24-Form Tai Chi Practice and Combat Techniques". The teaching team possesses extensive teaching experience, with more than half of them engaged in Tai Chi culture dissemination and instruction for over 20 years. The textbook

本教材以24式简化太极拳为教学载体，重在揭示太极拳各式的技击含义、实用技法，并将太极文化哲理贯穿始终。在学、练、悟等习练太极拳过程中，以学生为中心，以立德树人为宗旨，培养学生对太极拳和太极文化的喜爱与认同。作为规范的高校太极拳教材，融入丰富的太极拳教学与实战经验，引申相关理论，将太极拳动作、劲法、呼吸、实战运用等相关内容融为一体。

本教材是中国大学MOOC、国家一流课程“24式太极拳习练及实战技法”的配套教材。教学团队具有丰富的教学经验，一半以上的人已从事太极文化传播和教学20多年。教材以实践环节为主，尤其增加了传统养生与实战内容，给教学提供了非常有价值的创新理念；将科学研究成果、实战经验引

primarily focuses on practical exercises, particularly emphasizing traditional health preservation and combat content, providing valuable innovative practices in teaching. It incorporates scientific research achievements and combat experience into classroom instruction, enriching the teaching content and highlighting the uniqueness of the textbook.

入课堂教学，丰富了教学内容、凸显了教材的特色。

First, combining skill transmission with cultural inheritance to achieve idcological and political education.

第一，技能传授与文化传承相结合，实现课程思政。

Adhering to the concept of cultural inheritance, the construction of the curriculum's connotation is deepened by emphasizing cultural infiltration and cultivation throughout the process of skill transmission. Traditional cultural interpretations are added to the explanation of technical movements, principles of techniques, and the understanding of techniques, enabling students to deeply grasp the profound cultural connotations of "harmony in dealing with affairs" "distinguishing right from wrong" "tolerance and humility", and "using softness to overcome hardness" while learning the skills. This achieves an organic integration of skill transmission with cultural inheritance, as well as a perfect combination of skill learning and ideological and political education.

秉承文化传承理念，深化课程内涵建设，在技能传授的过程中注重文化渗透和文化培养。在技术动作和技术原理讲解、招式感悟等部分增加传统文化阐释，使学生在技能学习过程中体悟太极拳技术动作中所蕴含的"和谐处事""明辨是非""包容谦让""以柔克刚"深厚文化内涵，实现了技能传授与文化传承的有机结合，以及技能学习与课程思政的完美结合。

Second, combining routine learning with practical application to demonstrate the application of knowledge.

第二，套路学习与实践应用相结合，体现学以致用。

The teaching philosophy of "integrating practice and combat, form and application" is emphasized, whereby the complete set of

24-Form Tai Chi standardized movements is taught, while simultaneously integrating scenarios and techniques for practical combat applications, breathing and force, striking positions and timing throughout the entire teaching process. This allows students to comprehend the combat principles of "drawing in, emptying, adhering, and issuing" inherent in the technical movements, and reinforce the basic principles and norms of "heart and intent alignment" "intent and *qi* integration" "*qi* and force integration" "hand and foot coordination" "elbow and knee coordination" and "shoulder and hip coordination" during practical applications. It achieves an automatic integration of routine learning with practical application.

Third, combining talent cultivation with social service to enhance social impact.

Innovative teaching models serve the realization of two major functions: "talent cultivation" and "cultural inheritance" in higher education. Focusing on the real needs of Tai Chi enthusiasts in society, contributions are made to the promotion and popularization of Tai Chi, while also fulfilling the responsibility of "social service" in universities.

Fourth, combining domestic and international dissemination to expand the scope of promotion.

Adhering to the belief that "Tai Chi is both Chinese and global", opportunities arisc in the post-pandemic era where people worldwide have a strong desire for fitness and diverse means of exercise. Building upon the completion of teaching for

突出"练打结合、体用兼备"的教学理念,在教授24式太极拳整套规范动作的前提下,将太极拳24个技术动作实战应用的场景与技巧、呼吸与劲力、技击部位与时机等元素贯穿于整个教学过程,让学生在技术动作学习中体会技术动作本身蕴含的"引进落空合击出"技击原理,在实战应用中强化技术动作"心与意合""意与气合""气与力合""手与脚合""肘与膝合""肩与胯合"的基本原理和基本规范,实现了套路学习与实战应用的有机结合。

第三,人才培养与社会服务相结合,提高社会效应。

创新授课模式,服务高校"人才培养"和"文化传承"两大功能的实现;聚焦社会太极拳爱好者的现实需求,对太极拳的推广和普及做出了贡献,同时也担起了高校"社会服务"的职责。

第四,国内传播与国际传播相结合,扩大传播范围。

domestic university students and social Tai Chi enthusiasts, attention is now focused on the urgent demand for Tai Chi courses among international populations. The textbook continuously improves its content and presentation, incorporating bilingual (Chinese and English) elements, thereby broadening avenues for the international dissemination of Tai Chi and meeting the needs of international learners, thus assuming the responsibility of "internationalization" in universities. This achieves an automatic combination of domestic and international dissemination.

This textbook can be effectively utilized through a combination of online teaching and offline learning, as well as the integration of theory and practice, to fully stimulate students' interest in learning and subtly cultivate their scientific research and innovation abilities. Analyzing the practice of Tai Chi from a fresh perspective, it combines the fundamental knowledge of Tai Chi practice with the scientific theories it embodies. Through the course, students will acquire relevant knowledge and scientific principles of Tai Chi practice, experiencing the unique charm of Tai Chi.

The book was edited by Pro. Yu Shihai, the English part was translated by Associate Pro. Xu Tuo from institute of Foreign Languages, Nantong University, and the ideological and political part was edited by Pro. Sun Guozhi from institute of Marxism, Nantong University. The final draft of the book was compiled by Pro. Yu Shihai. The textbook consists of five chapters, with

始终坚持"太极拳是中国的也是世界的"的理念,后疫情时代各国民众健身意愿强烈和健身手段需求多元的现实机遇,在完成国内高校学生和社会太极拳爱好者群体教学的基础上,聚焦国际民众对太极拳课程的迫切需求,不断完善优化教材内容和表现形式,采用中英文双语,为太极拳的国际传播拓宽了途径,满足了国际民众的需求,担起了高校"国际化"的重担,实现了国内传播和国际传播有机结合。

本教材可以通过线上教学和线下学习相结合、理论与实践相结合的方式,充分激发学生的学习兴趣,潜移默化地培养学生的科学研究和创新能力。从全新的视角剖析太极拳运动,将太极拳运动的基本知识和所蕴含的科学理论相结合,学生通过课程学习,掌握太极拳运动的相关知识和科学规律,体会到太极拳运动独特的魅力。

online learning videos and post-lesson exercises accompanying the important knowledge points covered in the first three chapters, ensuring the seamless integration of online and offline resources. The last two chapters are about the competition rules of the Chinese College Students Tai Chi Pushing Hand Championship, which helps more college students understand the competition rules, and encourages more college students and overseas students to participate in the competition, so as to achieve the effect of promoting training through competition.

全书由於世海教授担任主编，英文部分由南通大学外国语学院徐托副教授翻译，课程思政部分由南通大学马克思主义学院孙国志教授参编，全书最后由於世海教授统稿。本教材共有五个章节，前三章节的重要知识点均配有线上学习视频及课后习题，使得线上线下有机结合；后两章为中国大学生太极推手锦标赛竞赛规则，让更多大学生能了解比赛规则，鼓励更多大学生朋友及留学生参加比赛，从而达到以赛促练的效果。

During the writing process of this textbook, numerous resources from renowned Tai Chi experts were consulted, and significant support was received from sister institutions. Sincere gratitude is expressed to them. Due to limitations in the author's expertise, there may be inadequacies in the book. Constructive criticism and feedback from readers are earnestly welcomed.

本教材在编写的过程中，参阅了许多太极名家的资料，得到了兄弟院校的大力支持，在此表示衷心的感谢。限于编者水平，书中有不妥之处，恳请广大读者给予批评指正。

Author
May 28, 2023

编 者
2023 年 5 月 28 日

太极拳课程简介

目　录

第一章　太极拳基础知识篇

Chapter 1: Fundamentals of Tai Chi Chuan

第一节　太极拳的起源

Section 1: The Origin of Tai Chi Chuan

Ⅰ. The Etymology of the Term "Tai Chi"

The term "Tai Chi" is familiar to many people, but what exactly is "Tai Chi" and what does it entail?

When did the term "Tai Chi" first appear?

The term "Tai Chi" is mentioned in various pre-Qin classics, including the *Book of Documents*, *Mozi*, *Zhuangzi*, and *Yizhuan*". In the *Book of Documents—Hong Fan*, it states, "The first is the Five Elements, the second is the reverent use of the Five Affairs, the third is the agricultural use of the Eight Policies, the fourth is the coordinated use of the Five Principles, and the fifth is the constructive use of the Supreme Ultimate..." Kong Yingda's commentary explains that "Supreme" means

一、太极一词的来源

对于"太极"这个词语，很多人都不陌生。但是，到底什么是"太极"，"太极"的内涵又是什么呢？

我们需要知道"太极"一词最早出现于何时？

先秦典籍中"太极"一词一共出现在四处，分别是《尚书》《墨子》《庄子》和《易传》。《尚书·洪范》有："初一曰五行，次二曰敬用五事，次三曰农用八政，次四曰协用五纪，次五曰建用皇极……"，孔颖达疏："皇，大也"。所以，"皇极"就是"大极"也就是"太极"。《墨子·非攻上》："禹既已克有三苗，焉磨为山川，别物上下，卿制大极，而神民不违，天下乃静，则此禹之所以征有苗也。"前两者对于"太极"一词还没有明确地指出，而在之后的《庄子·大宗师》"在太极之先

"Great" . Therefore, "Supreme Ultimate" is equivalent to "Great Ultimate," which is "Tai Chi." In the *Mozi—Against Offensive Warfare*, it states, "Since Yu had already conquered the Three Miao, why did he bother with smoothing the mountains, rivers, and organizing the world above and below? It is for the grand extreme of governance, so that the divine people do not go against it, and when the world is calm, it is because Yu was subduing the Miao" . The first two sources do not explicitly indicate the term "Tai Chi" , but it is clearly mentioned in the following sentence from the *Zhuangzi—The Great Master*: "Existing before Tai Chi, yet not reaching great heights; existing below tho Six Fxtremes, yet not sinking deep" . However, the most widely cited source of the term "Tai Chi" is from *the Book of Changes—Appended Remarks*: "The Great Extreme produced the Two Elementary Forms. These Two Elementary Forms produced the Four Emblematic Symbols,which again produce the Eight Trigrams. The Eight Trigrams determine good and bad fortune, and good and bad fortune gives birth to the great achievement."

而不为高,在六极之下而不为深"一句话中则将"太极"一词明确提出。而现在最广为流传也是学者引述最多的"太极"一词的出处,则是出自《周易·系辞》:"是故《易》有太极,是生两仪,两仪生四象,四象生八卦。八卦定吉凶,吉凶生大业。"

Thus, it is generally believed that "Tai Chi" was first mentioned in the *Zhuangzi* and gradually became known through the *Yizhuan*.

因此,一般意义上认为,"太极"最早出自《庄子》,在《易传》中"太极"一词逐渐广为人知。

Ⅱ. The Connotation of Tai Chi

二、太极的内涵

Tai Chi generally refers to two major categories: Tai Chi philosophy and Tai Chi Chuan.

太极一般指太极哲学和太极拳两大类。

Tai Chi philosophy dates back to legendary times. According to legend, "In ancient times, Bao Xi, the ruler of the world, observed the phenomena in the sky when looking up, and the principles on earth when looking down. He observed the patterns of birds and beasts and the appropriateness of the land. He observed himself closely and observed things from a distance, thus creating the Eight Trigrams". The study of Tai Chi philosophy focuses on exploring the cosmogony of Tai Chi in the *Yizhuan*. Different scholars in different dynasties have their own research theories.

太极哲学存在时间可推至传说时代，相传"古者，包牺氏之王天下也，仰则观象于天，俯则观法于地，观鸟兽之文与地之宜，近取诸身，远取诸物，于是始作八卦"。太极哲学的研究是基于《易传》中太极宇宙生成论而探讨的。在不同的朝代，不同的学者有其不同的研究理论。

When Tai Chi philosophy is combined with different disciplines, it gives rise to new things with Tai Chi philosophical significance, forming new cultural groups. For example, the combination of the *yin-yang* and Five Elements theories in Tai Chi philosophy with traditional Chinese medicine forms the theory of Five Elements and Five Organs; the combination of the harmonization of *yin* and *yang* in Tai Chi with alchemy forms the study of Neidan; the combination of the Tai Chi diagram in Tai Chi with Taoism forms the Tai Chi *yin-yang* fish diagram, and so on. Among the various cultural exchanges, the most successful and representative combination is that of Tai Chi philosophy and martial arts, giving rise to the well-known Tai Chi Chuan.

当太极哲学与不同的学科结合，就形成了具有太极哲学含义的新事物，从而形成新的文化群，如太极哲学中的阴阳五行与中医结合，就形成了五行五脏理论；太极中的阴阳调和与丹药结合，就形成了内丹学；太极中的太极图与道教结合，就形成了太极阴阳鱼图等。在众多文化交流中，最为成功也是最具有代表性的就是太极哲学和拳术的结合，形成了广为人知的太极拳。

Currently, the term "Tai Chi" primarily refers to Tai Chi Chuan (*taijiquan*). The exact birth time of Tai Chi Chuan cannot

现在意义上的"太极"一词主要指太极拳。太极拳诞生的时间具体不可考，但有实物的记载应为明朝王宗岳《太极拳论》为开端。严格来说，太极拳也是太极哲学文化圈

be determined, but the recorded evidence suggests that it originated with Wang Zongyue's *Tai Chi Chuan Treatise* during the Ming Dynasty. Strictly speaking, Tai Chi Chuan is also a materialized derivative within the Tai Chi philosophical and cultural sphere, belonging to Tai Chi philosophy. However, due to Tai Chi Chuan being one of the most widely practiced sports worldwide today, it is well-known. Furthermore, Tai Chi Chuan is closely integrated with Tai Chi philosophy, which can best embodies the philosophical connotations of Tai Chi. Therefore, Tai Chi Chuan gradually became synonymous with the term "Tai Chi" in the course of historical development, becoming a representative synonym for Tai Chi.

Tai Chi Chuan also combines with other disciplines or cultures to form the Tai Chi Chuan cultural group. Tai Chi Chuan culture is a recently emerging cultural term and phenomenon. Generally speaking, Tai Chi Chuan culture revolves around Tai Chi Chuan as the main body, combining aspects such as medical skills, guiding techniques, health preservation, religion, government policies, and tourism to form a culture. Examples include Tai Chi Chuan health preservation, Tai Chi Chuan music, Tai Chi Chuan summer camps, all of which are cultural products centered around Tai Chi Chuan. It is not difficult to observe that Tai Chi Chuan culture is mostly combined with current trends and demands, encompassing diverse content, and involving various fields.

下的一个实体化衍生物,从属于太极哲学。但是,由于太极拳是当今全世界参与人数最多的运动项目之一,广为人知。同时,太极拳与太极哲学结合最为紧密,最能体现太极哲学内涵的事物,故在时代发展之中太极拳逐渐和"太极"一词等同,成为太极的代名词。

太极拳也会和其他学科或文化结合,形成太极拳文化群,太极拳文化是最近出现的一个新的文化名词和文化现象。一般来说,太极拳文化是以太极拳为主体,结合医术、导引术、养生术、宗教、政府政策、旅游等方面所形成的文化。如太极拳养生、太极拳音乐、太极拳夏令营等,都是围绕太极拳展开的文化产品。不难发现,太极拳文化大多都与当下的流行和需求相结合,内容庞杂,且涉及各个领域。

Therefore, the term "Tai Chi" has both broad and narrow meaning. In a narrow sense, it mainly refers to Tai Chi philosophy and Tai Chi Chuan. In a broad sense, it represents a cultural symbol, a cultural group formed by the combination of Tai Chi philosophy and Tai Chi Chuan with different cultures. Therefore, when studying Tai Chi, one should understand it from both the philosophical meaning of Tai Chi and the aspect of Tai Chi Chuan.

所以,"太极"一词有广义和狭义两类。狭义上说,它多指太极哲学和太极拳。广义上来说,它是一种文化符号,是太极哲学与太极拳结合不同的文化而形成的文化群,故我们研究太极时应从太极的哲学含义以及太极拳两个方面去理解。

Ⅲ. The Emergence of Tai Chi Chuan

三、太极拳的产生

Tai Chi existed as a philosophical concept before the Ming Dynasty. However, Wang Zongyue, a martial artist from Shanxi during the Ming Dynasty, first used the concepts of Tai Chi and *yin-yang* philosophy to explain the principles of martial arts, thus giving birth to Tai Chi Chuan.

太极在明朝之前都是作为哲学的概念存在,然而明代山西武术家王宗岳首先用太极阴阳哲学概念来解释拳理,故名太极拳。

Looking at the history of Tai Chi Chuan, it is difficult to trace its exact origins. Generally speaking, there are six theories regarding the origins of Tai Chi Chuan.

纵观太极拳的历史,追其源头,我们难以考证。一般来说,太极拳的源头有五种说法。

The first theory attributes it to Cheng Lingxi of the Liang Dynasty. Cheng, a disciple of Han Gong, supposedly renamed Tai Chi Chuan as "*xiaojiutian*"("Small Nine Heavens"). The evidence for this theory lies in the similarity between the names of Tai Chi Chuan techniques mentioned in Cheng's writings, such as "Single Whip" "Lifting Hands" "Parting the Wild Horse's Mane",

其一为梁朝程灵洗。程为韩拱所传,将太极拳改名为"小九天",其证据就是其在书中所提的"单鞭""提手""野马分鬃""揽雀尾"等词和现在的太极拳招数名称相似。

and "Grasping the Sparrow's Tail", and the names of modern Tai Chi Chuan movements.

The second theory involves Xu Xuanping of the Tang Dynasty. In Xu's poem called *The Eight Characters Song*, there are verses that closely resemble the principles of modern Tai Chi Chuan, such as "Ward off, Roll back, Press, and Push are rare skills in the world. Ten practitioners, none understand. If one can be light and nimble yet firm and solid, sticking, adhering, connecting, and following without fear, then they will excel in Plucking, Splitting, Elbow Strikes, and Shouldering".

其二为唐朝许宣平,其所传的《八字歌》中有"掤捋挤按世界稀,十个艺人十不知,若能轻灵并坚硬,粘黏连随俱无疑,采挒肘靠更出奇"。与现代所说的太极拳的四正"掤、捋、挤、按",四隅"采、挒、肘、靠",以及基本原则"粘、黏、连、随"如出一辙。

The third theory associates Tai Chi Chuan with Hu Jingzi of the Tang Dynasty, who also mentioned techniques similar to Tai Chi Chuan.

其三为唐朝胡镜子,他也提到了类似太极拳的技法。

The fourth theory attributes the creation of Tai Chi Chuan to Zhang Sanfeng of the Ming Dynasty. It is widely believed in folklore that Zhang Sanfeng was the founder of Tai Chi Chuan, but there is a lack of concrete evidence, and many consider it a myth.

其四为明朝张三丰。民间盛传"张三丰创太极拳"可以作为其中一个依据,但缺少实证,多为神话故事。

It can be said that the first four theories laid the foundation for the basic principles, techniques, and theories of Tai Chi Chuan, but they did not provide a specific name for it. The explicit mention of the term "Tai Chi Chuan" came from Wang Zongyue in his work *Tai Chi Chuan Treatise* during the Ming Dynasty.

可以说,前四者已经形成了太极拳的一些基本法则、技术、理论,但并未对其有一个具体的名称定位。而明确提出太极拳一词的则是明代王宗岳的《太极拳论》。

The fifth theory involves the creation of Tai Chi Chuan by Chen Wangting in the late Ming Dynasty and early Qing Dynasty. According to Tang Hao, a Chinese martial arts historian, Chen Wangting from Wen County, Henan, during the late Ming Dynasty and early Qing Dynasty, was the earliest known practitioner of Tai Chi Chuan. He integrated ancient health cultivation methods, meridian theories, studied the *Huangting Jing* of Daoism, referenced Qi Jiguang's *Boxing Manual*, and incorporated various techniques to create the Chen-style Tai Chi Chuan. However, this theory can also be questioned as it contradicts the relatively comprehensive and modern technical system of Tai Chi Chuan that existed during the Tang Dynasty. Additionally, in the mid-Qing Dynasty, there were already significant divergences within Tai Chi Chuan, which goes against the general development pattern of things. Usually, differentiation occurs when a thing has reached a state of completeness, and it takes time for formation to differentiation. Therefore, the claim of Chen Wangting's initial creation also needs to be examined.

其五是明末清初的陈王廷创太极拳，据中国武术史学家唐豪考证，最早传习太极拳的是明末清初河南温县的陈王廷。他结合古代的导引养生术和经络学说，研究道家的《皇庭经》，参照戚继光的《拳经》，博采众长，加以继承和创新，创编了陈氏太极拳。不过此种说法也有所牵强，毕竟太极拳在唐朝已有相对完备和现代的技术体系。其次，清中期就有太极拳分流现象严重，根据事物的一般发展规律来说，只有当事物发展走向完备之时，才有基础和条件进行分化，而且从形成到分化需要一定的时间。这种短时期的分化在时间上有所相悖，故而以陈初创的认定也需要推敲。

第二节 太极拳的流派

Section 2: Schools of Tai Chi

The division of Tai Chi primarily began in the late Qing Dynasty. It is mainly based on the existing five major styles: Chen-style

太极拳的分流主要是从清末开始的。主要以现存的五大种类为分流基础，即陈式太极拳、杨式太极拳、武式太极拳、吴式太极拳以及孙式太极拳。

Tai Chi, Yang-style Tai Chi, Wu-style Tai Chi, Wu (Hao)-style Tai Chi, and Sun-style Tai Chi.

Ⅰ. Cheng-Style Tai Chi

Chen-style Tai Chi founded by Chen Wangting (Figure 1-1) (approximately 1600—1680), it was perfected and further developed by the 14th generation inheritor, Chen Changxing. The practice style and movement characteristics of Chen-style Tai Chi are characterized by coiling, folding, relaxation, elasticity, alternating fast and slow movements, a combination of softness and hardness, continuous and seamless flow, and unity in execution. It resembles the surging of rivers and possesses a grand momentum, akin to a playful dragon in water. The core lies in the concept of "coiling". Coiling of the body, hands, legs, arms, and legs, with the whole body engaged in coiling. Therefore, it is said that Chen-style Tai Chi is characterized by its "coiling" technique. Internally, it involves the movement of intention and energy, while externally, it involves spiral coiling movements. It emphasizes maintaining a relaxed and elongated posture with the crown of the head lifted and sinking the energy, leading to the rotation of the upper body through waist rotation and the rotation of the lower body through hip rotation, allowing the limbs to connect and penetrate through coordinated winding and unwinding. Chen-style Tai Chi includes both fast and slow

图 1-1 陈王廷

一、陈式太极拳

陈式太极拳创始人陈王廷(图 1-1)(约1600—1680),由第十四代传人陈长兴完备并后专精于太极拳。陈氏太极拳的演练风格和运动特点为缠绕折叠,松活弹抖,快慢相间,刚柔相济,连绵不断,一气呵成,如滔滔江河奔腾不息,气势恢宏,又似游龙戏水怡然自得。其核心就在于"自缠",身缠、手缠、足缠、臂缠、腿缠,周身缠,故有陈氏太极拳乃"缠"法也之说。其在内是意气运动,在外是螺旋缠绕运动。强调在意识主持下,头顶、气沉,放长身肢,通过旋腰转脊带动上肢旋膀转腕,带动下肢旋胯转踝,使肢体在顺逆缠绕中,促成内外相合,节节贯穿。陈式太极拳的动作有快、有慢,一般发劲时和转换时快,动作过渡时慢,陈式太极拳有刚有柔,一般动作的终点刚,过程柔。全套动作在快慢、刚柔、开合、曲直中相互依存、互相转化。

movements. Generally, the exertion of force and transitions are performed quickly, while the movements during transition periods are slow. It combines both hardness and softness, with the final point of a movement being firm and the process being gentle. The complete set of movements interdependently transform between fast and slow, hard and soft, opening and closing, and curved and straight.

图 1-2 杨露禅

Ⅱ. Yang-Style Tai Chi

Yang-style Tai Chi founded by Yang Luchan (Figure 1-2) (1799—1872), who learned from Chen Changxing and passed it down to his son, Yang Jianhou, and his grandson, Yang Chengfu, completing three generations. The structure of Yang-style Tai Chi is expansive and graceful, with a central and upright posture. The movements are smooth, natural, continuous, and solid yet relaxed. It transitions from loose to yielding, and it achieves a harmonious unity, as if floating on a lake with a light and steady presence. The practice method is concise and widely appreciated by the general public, resulting in its broad dissemination. The movements of Yang-style Tai Chi should flow continuously like the mighty Yangtze River. Each movement seamlessly connects to the next, maintaining an unbroken flow. The mental intention also requires a unified execution.

二、杨式太极拳

杨式太极拳创始人杨露禅(图 1-2)(1799—1872),学于陈长兴,后传于其子杨建候以及其孙杨澄甫,三代完备。杨式太极拳拳架舒展优美、身法中正、动作和顺、平正朴实、由松入柔、刚柔相济,一气呵成,犹如湖中泛舟轻灵沉着兼而有之,练法简洁,深受一般大众的喜爱,故而流传最广。杨式太极拳动作要求如长江大河,滔滔不绝。此动作之完成,乃下一动作开端,绵延相续,心法上亦要求一气呵成。

图 1-3 武禹襄

Ⅲ. Wu-Style Tai Chi

Wu-style Tai Chi founded by Wu Yuxiang (Figure 1-3) (1812—1880), who learned from Yang Luchan and later passed it down to his nephew, Li Yishe. It was then transmitted to Shanghai, where it was renamed Hao-style Tai Chi under the fourth generation inheritor, Hao Yueru. Wu-style Tai Chi is one of the five major traditional Tai Chi styles. Its principles are rich, complete, profound, and delicate. It emphasizes the pursuit of Tai Chi (internal form) as the main focus, employing internal power through the coordination of intention and breath. The characteristic of Wu-style Tai Chi is "changing according to the opponent's movements and borrowing their strength" by utilizing variations in mental intention to control external movements. It emphasizes the use of internal power without revealing external appearances, achieving

三、武式太极拳

武式太极拳创始人武禹襄(图 1-3)(1812—1880),学丁杨露禅,后传于其外甥李亦畬,至第四代郝月如传至上海,改为郝式太极拳。武氏太极拳是传统太极拳五大流派之一,其理法原理丰富完整又邃密细腻,以求太极(内形)为主,走内劲,以意行气,练精、气、神三者合一。其技艺特点是"因敌变化、借力打人",用意气的变换来支配外形的运动,强调走内劲而不露外形,达到人为我制,而我不为人制的神奇境界。武氏太极拳拳架既不同于陈氏太极拳大架与小架,也不同于杨氏太极拳,其拳架姿势紧凑,动作舒缓,步法严格分虚实,胸、腹部进退皆旋转,身体中正,用内动的虚实来支配外形(叫内气潜转),左右手各管半边,不相逾越,出手不过足尖,原来有跳跃动作,到第四代郝月如改为不纵不跳。

a remarkable state where one can control others while being immune to their control. The framework of Wu-style Tai Chi differs from both Chen-style Tai Chi (large and small frames) and Yang-style Tai Chi. Its stance is compact, movements are gentle, and footwork strictly distinguishes between emptiness and fullness. The chest and abdomen rotate during advances and retreats, maintaining an upright posture, while using internal movement to control external appearances (refcrred to as the covert transformation of internal energy). Each hand manages its own half, without crossing over, and the hands do not extend beyond the toes. Originally, there were jumping movements, but they were eliminated in the Wu- (Hao-) style passed down by Wu Yuxiang's fourth-generation inheritor, Hao Yueru.

Ⅳ. Wu-Style Tai Chi

Wu-style Tai Chi founded by Wu Quanyou (Figure 1-4) (1834—1902), who learned from Yang Luchan. It was later passed down to his son, Wu Jianquan, who made modifications to form a distinct lineage. Wu-style Tai Chi is known for its softness, with movements that are light, natural, and continuously connected. The form transitions from an open state to a compact state, maintaining compactness without appearing restricted. The pushing hands techniques are precise, delicate, and characterized by stillness and non-superfluous movements. It is renowned for its emphasis on softness.

图 1-4　吴全佑

四、吴式太极拳

吴式太极拳创始人吴全佑(1834—1902),学于杨露禅。后传于其子吴鉴泉加以修改形成一派。吴式太极拳以柔化著称,动作轻松自然,连续不断,拳式小巧灵活。拳架由开展而紧凑,紧凑中不显拘谨。推手动作严密、细腻,守静而不妄动,亦以柔化见长。

图 1–5 孙禄堂

V. Sun-Style Tai Chi

Sun-style Tai Chi founded by Sun Lutang (Figure 1-5) (1860—1933), who initially learned Wu-style Tai Chi from Hao Weizhen. Afterward, Sun Lutang studied Xingyiquan (Form-Intention Fist) from Li Kuiyuan and Baguazhang (Eight Trigram Palm) from Cheng Tinghua, integrating them into Tai Chi to create Sun-style Tai Chi. The distinctive features of Sun-style Tai Chi are progressive footwork and corresponding body movements, agile actions, a rounded and compact structure, and continuous flow, resembling flowing clouds and uninterrupted movements. Each turn of the body transitions smoothly between opening and closing. The essence of Sun-style Tai Chi lies in the integration of the unity of internal and external aspects from Xingyiquan and the unity of movement and stillness from Bagua-Zhang into the harmonious state of Tai Chi. When practicing the form, the center of gravity remains stable without rising or falling, and there is no swaying from side to side. This is achieved by constantly shifting

五、孙式太极拳

孙武太极拳创始人孙禄堂(图 1-5)(1860—1933),学于武式太极拳郝为真。孙禄堂在向李魁垣学习形意拳、程廷华学习八卦掌之后,结合太极拳,创孙式太极拳。孙氏太极拳的风格特点主要是:进步必跟、退步必随、动作敏捷、圆活紧凑,犹如行云流水,连绵不断,每左右转身以开合相接。孙氏太极拳最本质的特点是将形意拳之内外合一和八卦拳之动静合一融蓄在太极拳的中和状态之中。走架时重心无上下起伏、无左右晃动的问题,通过活步使重心不断地在转换当中。孙氏太极拳,从起式到收式,各种动作要求中正平稳、舒展圆活、紧凑连贯、一气呵成,使全身内外平均发展,一动无不动,一静无不静。

the center of gravity through agile stepping. Sun-style Tai Chi requires movements to be performed with balance, flexibility, compactness, and continuity, harmonizing the development of the whole body, both internally and externally, achieving unity in both motion and stillness.

From this, we can roughly infer the process of the division of Tai Chi. It began during the Tang Dynasty when the basic theorics and technical systems of Tai Chi gradually took shape. By the early Ming Dynasty, Tai Chi was defined, and numerous theoretical writings emerged. Towards the end of the Ming Dynasty and the beginning of the Qing Dynasty, Tai Chi, represented by Chen-style, experienced further divergence. Eventually, the division occurred explosively and peacefully during the late Qing Dynasty.

由此,我们大概推断出太极拳的分流过程,即在唐朝开始,太极拳的基本理论和技术体系已经逐渐完成。到明初之时,太极拳定性,并且出现大量的理论论著。到明末清初,太极拳以陈氏为代表,出现分流,至清末,则以爆发式、平方式的方式进行分流。

第三节 练习太极拳身体基本姿势要求

Section 3: Basic Body Posture Requirements for Practicing Tai Chi

When practicing Tai Chi, there are high requirements for the posture and form of various body parts, as outlined below.

练习太极拳时对身体各部位的姿势形态有较高的要求,具体如下。

Ⅰ. Head

一、头部

The posture of the head is strictly regulated during Tai Chi practice. Terms such

练习太极拳时,对头部姿势的要求是很严格的。所谓“头顶悬”“虚领顶劲”,或“提

as "suspended headtop" or "empty neck and lifted crown" emphasize that practitioners should lift their heads upward, avoiding stiffness in the neck muscles and any tilting or shaking of the head. The movements of the head and neck should be coordinated and consistent with the rotation and movement of the torso. The face should be natural, the chin slightly tucked in, the mouth gently closed, and the tongue lightly pressed against the roof of the mouth to enhance saliva secretion.

顶""吊顶"的说法,都是要求练习者头向上顶,避免颈部肌肉硬直,更不要东偏西歪或自由摇晃。头颈动作应随着身体位置和方向的变换,与躯干的旋转上下连贯协调一致。面部要自然,下颌向里收回,口自然合闭,舌上卷舔住上腭,以加强唾液的分泌。

The gaze of the eyes should follow the body's movements, focusing on the leading hand (or the trailing hand during backward movements) or looking straight ahead. Avoid furrowing the brow or staring angrily, as well as closing or wandering eyes. During the practice, strive for a natural expression, maintain concentration, as lack of focus can affect the effectiveness of the exercise.

眼神要随着身体的转动,注视前手(后划时候看后手)或平视前方,既不可皱眉怒目,也不要随意闭眼或精神涣散。打拳时,神态力求自然,注意力一定要集中,否则会影响锻炼效果。

Ⅱ. Torso

二、躯干部

1. Chest and Back

Tai Chi emphasizes "hollow chest, raised back" or "contained in the chest, movement in the shoulders." This means that during the practice, the chest should not protrude forward, but also should not excessively collapse inward. It should remain in a natural state. The muscles of the back should stretch and expand as the arms extend, while the chest muscles should remain relaxed and not tense. This achieves

1. 胸背

太极拳要领中指出要"含胸拔背",或者"含蓄在胸,运动在两肩",意思是说在锻炼过程中要避免胸部外挺,但也不要过分内缩,应顺其自然。"含胸拔背"是互相联系的,背部肌肉随着两臂伸展动作,尽量地舒展开,同时注意胸部肌肉要自然松弛,不可使其紧张,这样胸就有了"含"的意思,背也有了"拔"的形式,从而也可免除胸肋间的紧张,呼吸调节也应自然。

the "hollow" quality of the chest and the "raised" form of the back, preventing tension in the chest and intercostal muscles and allowing for natural breathing.

2.Waist and Spine

The waist and spine play a crucial role in maintaining proper posture during daily activities and in Tai Chi practice. The body should be upright, balanced, and comfortable. Past sayings such as "the waist is the primary controller" or "keep your attention on the waist, with the abdomen relaxed and the *qi* rising" "highlight the importance of the waist." The waist must provide support and act as an axis during body movements; otherwise, it is impossible to achieve a harmonious flow of *qi* throughout the body. During practice, whether advancing, retreating, or rotating, the waist should consciously relax and hang downward, aiding in the sinking of *qi*. Avoid forcefully thrusting the waist forward, as it may affect flexibility during transitions. By relaxing and hanging the waist, leg strength can be increased, providing stability and enabling rounded and complete movements.

The spine should maintain its natural alignment, neither intentionally flexed backward nor forward, nor tilted to the sides, to avoid unnecessary tension in the chest, ribcage, or abdominal muscles. By maintaining the balance and alignment of the spine through the relaxation of the waist, movements become light, agile, and stable. Thus, the waist and spine serve as the primary controllers in Tai Chi practice.

2. 腰脊

人体在日常生活中，行、站、坐、卧要想保持正确的姿势，腰脊起着主要作用。在练习太极拳的过程中、身体要求端正安舒，不偏不倚，腰部起着重要的作用。过去有人说“腰脊为第一之主宰”，又说“刻刻留心在腰间，腹内松静气腾然”“腰为车轴”等，都说明了如果腰部力量中断或在身体转动中起不了车轴作用，就不可能做到周身完整一气。练习时，无论是进退或旋转，凡是由虚而逐渐落实的动作，腰部都要有意识地向下松垂，以帮助气的下沉。注意腰腹不可用力前挺，以免影响转换时的灵活性。这样腰部向下松垂，可以增加两腿力量，使下盘得到稳固，使动作既圆活又完整。

在配合松腰的要领当中，脊椎骨要根据生理正常姿态竖起，不可因松腰而故意后屈、前挺或左右歪斜，以致造成胸肋或腹部肌肉的无谓紧张。通过腰部维护身体的重心，能使动作既轻灵又稳定。可见，腰脊是练太极拳的第一主宰。

3.Hips

The requirement for the hips during Tai Chi practice is to "sink" or "tuck under" to avoid protruding hips that disrupt the natural alignment of the body. During practice, attention should be paid to naturally relaxing the hips, avoiding unnecessary twisting or rotating. While adhering to the requirements of a relaxed waist and aligned spine, the muscles of the hips should consciously contract to maintain an upright posture. Similar to the requirement for the head, the control is achieved through conscious adjustment rather than forceful control.

3. 臀部

练太极拳时要求"垂臀"(或称"敛臀"),这是为了避免臀部凸出而破坏身体的自然形态。练习时,要注意臀部自然下垂,不要左右扭动。要在松腰、正脊的要求下,臀部肌肉要有意识地收敛,以维持躯干的正直。总之,垂臀和顶头的要求一样,应用意识调整,不是用力去控制。

Ⅲ. Legs

In Tai Chi practice, the transformation of weight distribution, the generation of power, and the stability of the entire body primarily rely on the legs. Therefore, it is essential to pay special attention to the shifting of the center of gravity, the placement of the feet, and the degree of knee flexion. As practitioners often say, "the roots are in the feet, power comes from the legs, controlled by the waist, and expressed through the fingers" . This demonstrates that the quality of leg movements and postures directly affects the correctness of the overall body posture. When moving the legs, it is important to relax the hip and knee joints, which ensures agility in stepping forward or backward. Footwork should be light and flexible. When advancing, the heel touches the ground first, and when retreating, the ball

三、腿部

在练习太极拳的过程中,进退的变换,发劲的根源和周身的稳定,主要在于腿部。因而,在锻炼时,要特别注意重心的移动、脚放的位置和腿弯的程度。练拳人常讲:"其根在脚,发于腿,主宰于腰,形于手指",可见腿部动作姿势的好坏,关系着周身姿势的正确与否。腿部活动时,首先要求胯和膝关节放松,这样可以保证进退灵便。脚的起落,要轻巧灵活;前进时脚跟先着地,后退时脚掌先着地,然后慢慢踏实。

of the foot touches the ground first, followed by a gradual solid placement of the foot.

Beginners often focus more on the upper body while neglecting the movements of the legs and feet, which can affect the learning of the entire Tai Chi form. It is crucial to recognize the importance of leg and foot movements in posture transitions. Mastery of various stepping patterns and footwork is necessary. During the practice of the form, attention must be given to the solidity and emptiness of leg movements. Except for the "commencing form" "closing form" and "cross-hands", avoid placing equal weight on both legs simultaneously. The concept of solidity and emptiness in leg movements means that if the weight is on the right leg, the right leg is solid, and the left leg is empty, and vice versa. However, to maintain body balance, the empty leg still serves as a pivot point (e.g., the front foot in an empty stance or the rear foot in a bow stance). Overall, it is important to distinguish between solidity and emptiness without making them absolute. This approach allows for flexible and stable transitions, alternating load and rest between the legs, and reducing muscle tension and fatigue.

初学的人,往往会感到顾了手又顾不了脚,而且大多数人只注意了上肢的动作,而忽略了腿脚的动作,以致影响了整个拳架的学习。应该充分认识腿脚动作在姿势变换中的重要性。认真学好各种步型步法。在练架子时,必须注意腿部动作的虚实,除“起势”“收势”和“十字手”外,避免体重同时落在两腿上。所谓腿部动作的落实,就是体重在右腿则右腿为实,左腿为虚;体重在左腿则左腿为实,右腿为虚。但是,为了维持身体平衡,虚脚还要起着一个支点的作用(如“虚步”的前脚和弓步的后脚)。总之,既要分清虚实,又不要绝对化。这样进退转换不仅动作灵活稳定,而且可使两腿轮换负荷与休息,减少肌肉的紧张和疲劳。

Ⅳ. Arms

In Tai Chi terminology, "sinking the shoulders, drooping the elbows" indicates the need to relax these two joints. The shoulder and elbow joints are interconnected;

四、臂部

太极拳术语中讲“沉肩坠肘”,就是要求这两个部位的关节放松。肩、肘两个关节是相关联的,能沉肩就能坠肘。运动时应经常注意肩关节松开下沉,并有意识地向外引申。

when the shoulders are relaxed, the elbows naturally drop. During movement, the shoulders should frequently be relaxed and allowed to sink down, while consciously extending outward.

The palms of the hands in Tai Chi should be slightly reserved when gathering, neither overly soft nor floating. When pushing forward, in addition to focusing on sinking the shoulders and drooping the elbows, the wrists should also be slightly downward but not excessively bent. Hand movements should be smooth and flexible. When striking with the palm, the hand should be natural, and the fingers should be extended slightly. The fist should be rclaxed, avoiding excessive force.

太极拳对手掌部位的要求是：凡是收掌的动作，手掌应微微含蓄，但又不可软化、漂浮；当手掌前推时，除了注意沉肩垂肘之外，同时手腕要微向下坐，但不可弯得太死。手法的屈伸翻转，要力求轻松灵活。出掌要自然，手指要舒展(微屈)。拳要松握，不要太用力。

The movements of the hands and shoulders should be coordinated. If the hands are overly extended forward, it can result in the arms being too straight, not meeting the requirements of “sinking the shoulders and drooping the elbows”. Conversely, if the shoulders and elbows are excessively relaxed, neglecting the forward extension of the hands, the arms can become too bent. Overall, the arms should maintain a certain curvature throughout the movements. Whether performing pushing or gathering actions, avoid sudden loss of strength to achieve a continuous and flowing, light yet solid, and flexible and natural rhythm.

手和肩的动作是完整一致的，如果手过度向前引申，就容易把手臂伸直，达不到“沉肩坠肘”的要求；而过分地沉肩坠肘，忽略了手地向前引申，又容易使臂部过于弯曲。总之，动作时，臂部始终要保持一定的弧度，做推掌、收掌动作都不要突然断劲，这样才能做到既有节奏又能连绵不断，轻而不浮、沉而不僵，灵活自然。

第四节　太极拳的运动特点

Section 4: Movement Characteristics of Tai Chi

The movements of Tai Chi are gentle, light, and slow. The motion is like pulling silk, with curves everywhere. It is neither fully extended nor fully contracted, exhibiting roundness and liveliness without stagnation. There is movement within stillness, and stillness within movement. The practitioner guides the movements with their consciousness, allowing the body to follow the intention. This is accompanied by even and elongated breathing. The entire sequence of movements flows continuously, like flowing clouds and flowing water, providing the whole body with uniform and coordinated activity.

太极拳的动作柔和、轻灵、缓慢，其运动如抽丝，处处有弧形，似展非展，圆活不滞，动中有静，静中有动。用意识引导动作，意到身随，配合均匀细长的呼吸，整套动作如行云流水，连绵不断，使全身上下得到均匀而协调的活动。

Ⅰ. Calm Mind and Relaxed Body

Calm mind and relaxed body are important characteristics that distinguish Tai Chi from other sports activities. Practicing Tai Chi requires concentrated thinking and wholehearted focus on the movements, achieving “concentration of spirit, tranquility of mind, focus of intention, and relaxation of body”. “Calm mind” is an essential principle in Tai Chi practice, requiring focused thinking and continuous guidance

一、心静体松

心静体松是太极拳运动区别于其他体育项目的重要特点之一。打太极拳要求思想集中，全神贯注于动作，做到“神聚、心静、意专、体松”。“心静”是练太极拳的重要原则，“心静”要求要专心，在练拳时，思想要集中，意识不断地引导动作，并且灵活变换，使任何动作都有一定的指向，不能顾此失彼；“心静”要有耐心，不可焦躁或心猿意马，否则动作方向、姿势不正确，就难以把太极拳学好、练好。“体松”是和心静同样重要的

of the movements with consciousness. It involves flexible variations and ensuring that each movement has a specific direction, without neglecting any aspect. "Calm mind" requires patience, avoiding impatience or distractions, as incorrect movement direction or posture can hinder the effective learning and practice of Tai Chi. "Relaxed body" is equally important and is an important measure to implement the principle of "using intention rather than force". During the practice, under the premise of a calm mind, the practitioner guides the relaxation of various organs, joints, and muscles throughout the body, making every effort to ensure that there is no unnecessary tension. By applying appropriate force and focusing the intention on the process of the movements, the actions are performed with moderate adaptation to the changes between substantial and insubstantial.

一个原则,是贯彻"用意不用力"的重要措施。运动时,在心静的前提下用意引导肢体内外各个器官、关节和肌肉的放松,逐步做到全身不该用力处毫不用力,内外各部分无一处不松,尽量使身体自然舒展而不僵硬。按照规矩用劲,以意贯注于动作过程之中,按照动作的虚实变化适度地完成动作。

Ⅱ. Lightness and Stability

Tai Chi practice requires light and agile movements with a stable center of gravity under the guidance of consciousness. "Lightness" is a necessary measure to ensure full relaxation throughout the body. It means that "every movement should be as light as possible." Only by minimizing effort, the movements become more flexible. Without lightness, relaxation cannot be achieved, and without relaxation, agility is hindered. Agility develops based on lightness and reaches a level of sensitivity where even a

二、轻灵沉稳

练太极拳要求在意识引导下动作轻灵、重心沉稳。"轻灵"是保证全身内外充分放松的必要措施。所谓"一举动,周身俱要轻灵",只有用力越少越好的、轻的练法,动作才能越练越灵活。不轻就不能松,不松就不能灵活。灵是在轻的基础上发展,方能达到"一羽不能加"的高度敏感的灵。"沉稳"是使上体端正舒适,保持下肢稳定,要求虚领、立身中正、气沉丹田、步似猫行。进退转换,要分清虚实,步随身腰变化,需稳健、轻灵、沉着。

feather cannot be added. "Stability" refers to maintaining an upright and comfortable upper body and stable lower limbs. It requires an empty and upright upper body, proper alignment, sinking the *qi* to the *dantian*, and stepping lightly like a cat. When transitioning between movements, it is necessary to distinguish between substantial and insubstantial, adapt the steps to the changes in the waist, and maintain stability, lightness, and composure.

Ⅲ. Softness and Slowness

The premise of "softness" is relaxation, which directly relates to relieving fatigue, accumulating strength, and improving endurance, speed, agility, and technique. During the practice, continuous relaxation is required under the guidance of a calm mind and intention throughout the body. Relaxation is an active and vigorous state of mind, rather than being absent-minded or passive. While practicing, it is essential to maintain an arc shape in the movements based on relaxation. "Slowness" is also an important characteristic of Tai Chi. It refers to a steady and balanced slowness, where muscles and joints do not contract or rotate at specific angles but engage in a series of static force exercises that involve various angles.

三、柔和缓慢

"柔和"的前提是要放松,放松对缓解疲劳、积蓄力量,以及提高耐力、速度、灵敏和技巧等,都有直接的关系。练习时,要求始终放松,在心静用意的前提下,引导全身放松。放松是用意的,是积极振作的,不是漫不经心、消极疲沓的。练习时,要在放松的基础上使两臂动作保持弧形,使两臂运动走弧线。"缓慢"也是太极拳的重要特点,它是一种平稳中正得缓慢,肌肉和骨节不是处在某一特定角度下收缩和旋转,而是用许多不同的角度完成一系列伸缩和旋转的静力性练习。

Ⅳ. Continuity and Roundness

The practice of Tai Chi requires the principles of "uninterrupted movement"

四、连贯圆活

练太极拳要求"一动无有不动""由脚而腿而腰,总须完整一气",要求做到上下相

and "maintaining a complete flow of energy from the feet to the legs to the waist". It emphasizes the need for interconnectedness, coherence, and fluidity in each movement. The practitioner must carefully analyze and comprehend the initiation and conclusion of each posture. When reaching a fixed position, they must have a deep sense of concentration, creating a state that seems to be paused yet still in motion. This seamless transition between movements is referred to as continuity. Continuity entails smoothly linking the preceding and subsequent movements, maintaining a slight sense of motion during the transition without stiffness or stagnation. There should be no pauses or interruptions. Movements should exhibit roundness, meaning they should be complete, flexible, and devoid of defects, sharp angles, or rigid changes. Changes should be executed with lightness, agility, and liveliness within a continuous arc-shaped motion.

随、节节贯穿的连贯圆活。每一势如何起、如何落,要仔细揣摩,到定势时必须意识贯注十分满足,似停非停,这种势与势之间的承接,就称作连贯。连贯就是要求上一动作和下一动作折叠地衔接起来,转接处微微贯动,不僵不滞,不能有停顿断续之处。动作要圆活,亦即动作要圆满、灵活,在一连贯的弧形动作中圆满得不凹不凸,无有缺陷,不起棱角,变动又非常轻灵活泼。圆满灵活运用到动作上,要求达到中正不偏、不越界限、不被压扁、走化粘依、不丢不顶、处处圆满灵活。

Ⅴ. Correct Body Alignment

The concept of "correct body alignment" in Tai Chi refers to being "neither biased nor leaning" and "maintaining a vertical alignment from top to bottom." The body alignment in Tai Chi emphasizes standing with an upright and comfortable posture, supporting all directions equally, and avoiding any imbalance or deviation. It aims to convey an image of being centered, graceful, well-organized, expansive, and flowing, in accordance with the static

五、身法中正

"身法中正"指的是"中正不偏""上下一条线"。太极拳的身法主要是"立身须中正安舒,支撑八面""不偏不倚,无过不及",处处不使身体各部位散漫失中。要表现出中正、大方、工整、舒展和流畅的形象,符合心静用意的静态要求。练习时不论前进、后退、左旋、右转,四肢动作不论如何转换,自头顶、躯干至会阴始终要形成一条直线,凡是身向前俯、后仰、左歪、右斜、失去重心垂直平衡的,都是不符合"中正不偏"的要求,都是身法上的缺点。"上下一条线"的关键在于用意识使脊柱保持垂直状态。太极拳

requirements of a tranquil mind. Whether moving forward, backward, turning left, or rotating right, regardless of the transformation of limb movements, a straight line must be maintained from the crown of the head to the perineum. Deviating from this vertical balance, such as leaning forward or backward, tilting to the left or right, or losing vertical equilibrium, contradicts the requirement of "neither biased nor leaning" and represents a flaw in body alignment. The key to maintaining the principle of "one line from top to bottom" lies in using consciousness to ensure the spine remains vertical. The lightness and roundness of Tai Chi body alignment rely on the coordinated movement and rotation of the waist, hips, and chest, enabling the body to maintain balance from any angle. Whether advancing, retreating, or rotating, regardless of the extension or contraction of the limbs, body alignment must remain centered. The correct alignment of the crown and the coccyx represents the central focus of proper body alignment in Tai Chi. However, without coordinating actions such as sinking the chest, raising the back, and sinking the *qi* to the *dantian*, the chest will become rigid and lack movement, and the legs will only rotate left or right in conjunction with the rotation of the waist, without the upward and downward curved movements of rising and falling. Proper alignment begins with the requirement of sinking the crown and maintaining an upright position, while sinking the coccyx acts as the guiding force for directing movements. Holding the chest

身法的轻灵、圆活，全凭腰、胯、胸的运转和协调动作，使得在任何角度上都能够保持全身的平衡；进退、旋转，不论手足如何伸缩，身法必须保持中正。虚灵顶劲和尾闾中正是太极拳身法中正不偏的标志。但如果没有含胸拔背和气沉丹田的协调动作，胸部就会僵硬地得不到运动，腿部也只有随着腰部的左旋右旋而左右旋转，得不到一升一降的上起下落的弧形运动。虚灵顶劲是身法中正的首要条件，尾闾中正作为动作定向的舵手，含胸拔背和气沉丹田是身法上须始终保持的，是气不上浮、重心稳定的关键。

inward, raising the back, and sinking the *qi* to the *dantian* are essential aspects to maintain body alignment, ensuring that the *qi* does not rise, and the center of gravity remains stable.

Ⅵ. Coordination and Integrity

The continuity and roundness of Tai Chi rely on the relaxed state of the muscles throughout the body. The entire musculature, under conscious control, engages in precise, coordinated, organized, and systematic movements that do not disrupt balance through the splitting forces generated by joint tensions. Instead, it seeks to find the unified force point for each movement within the interconnected sequence. This aspect of Tai Chi is known as symmetrical coordination. The inherent principles of symmetrical coordination in Tai Chi can be summarized in five aspects: intending to move upward must first involve downward intention; intending to move left must first involve a shift to the right; within forward movement, there must be support from behind; upward, downward, left, and right movements attract and connect with each other; pulling and stretching lead to lengthening, aiming for straightness within flexibility.

六、协调完整

太极拳的连贯圆活，是在肌肉放松的情况下，全身肌肉群在意识指挥下做精确严密的、有组织的、有规律的统一性运动，不使各关节拉力所产生的分力破坏平衡，而是在节节贯穿中求得每一动作的合力点。这在太极拳中称作对称协调。太极拳对称协调的内在规律，可以总结为五个方面：意欲向上，必先欲下；意欲向左，必先右去；前去之中，必有后撑；上下左右，相吸相系；对拉拔长，曲中求直。

Ⅶ. Natural Breathing

Natural breathing in Tai Chi occurs spontaneously in response to the changes in movement. Even those who initially

七、呼吸自然

太极拳呼吸是根据动作的变化而自然形成的，与动作配合不起来或用自然呼吸法的人，坚持长时间练拳，也会不自觉地使动

struggle to coordinate their breathing eventually unconsciously synchronize their breathing with their movements during long-term practice. The combination of opening and closing, emptiness and fullness, and breathing should occur naturally. When emptiness combines with being open, it represents the act of gathering and inhaling, while fullness combined with being closed signifies the act of releasing and exhaling. Each opening and closing corresponds to one inhalation and exhalation. Opening through inhalation and closing through exhalation are concepts based on the expansion and contraction of the thorax. Opening refers to the expansion, while closing refers to the contraction. Opening and closing are observable postural phenomena, emptiness and fullness pertain to the internal manifestations of lightness and sinking, and breathing is a natural physiological phenomenon. These three aspects, when closely integrated, constitute the comprehensive and unified approach of Tai Chi exercise, combining the cultivation of intention, *qi*, and physicality.

作和自然呼吸结合起来。开合、虚实与呼吸要自然结合，合和虚是蓄、吸，开和实是发、呼，一开一合就是一呼一吸。开吸合呼是以胸廓的扩张与收缩为开合的概念，胸廓扩张的动作为开；反之为合。开合是姿势上的现象，虚实是内劲的轻和沉的现象，呼吸是运动生理上的自然现象，三者密切地自然结合，构成了太极拳锻炼方法上练意、练气、练身三结合的整体性和内外统一性。

Ⅷ. Following Intentions with the Body

Any human action, including various physical exercises, requires conscious guidance, except for reflexive actions. The entire process of practicing Tai Chi also necessitates using consciousness (specifically, imaginative visualization) to direct movements and concentrate attention within the movements. The saying

八、意领身随

人体的任何动作(除反射性的动作外)，包括各种体育锻炼的动作，都需要经过意识的指挥。练习太极拳的全部过程，也要求用意识(指想象力)引导动作，把注意力灌注到动作中去。太极拳论说："神为主帅，身为驱使"，意动身随就是这个意思。

in Tai Chi states, "The spirit serves as the commander, and the body acts accordingly." Thus, "following intentions with the body" signifies this idea.

第五节 太极拳的健身功效

Section 5: Health Benefits of Tai Chi

The distinctive movement style and requirements of Tai Chi have significant health and therapeutic effects on various systems such as respiration, digestion, nervous system, and cardiovascular system. Its moderate exercise intensity and volume result in less drastic metabolic changes after practice, making it suitable for individuals of different physical constitutions and ages, especially those who are physically weak or suffering from chronic illnesses. Therefore, it is one of the preferred exercise programs for promoting nationwide fitness in our country.

太极拳的特殊运动方式与要求对呼吸、消化、神经、心血管等系统,有着较为显著的保健和医疗作用。其运动强度和运动量较为适中,练习后不易出现代谢机能的激烈变化,适合于不同体质和不同年龄的人们,特别是体弱及慢性病患者。因此,它也是我国推广全民健身运动的首选运动项目之一。

Ⅰ. Scientific breathing improves the function of the respiratory system

一、科学的呼吸方式,改善呼吸系统功能

Tai Chi emphasizes diaphragmatic breathing, whether through natural breathing or coordinated breathing with the movements. The breath is coordinated with mental focus, where inhalation guides the internal energy along the Governing Vessel (*dumai*) up the spine, and exhalation guides the internal energy down the Conception

太极拳强调腹式呼吸,不管是用自然呼吸还是拳势呼吸都强调腹式呼吸。呼吸还配合意念,就是吸气时内气沿脊椎督脉上行,呼气时内气沿前胸任脉下沉,小腹则是吸凸呼凹。合理地运用呼吸锻炼可以扩大肺活量。科学实验表明,肺活量的大小与力量的大小及生命长短成正比。诸如人体处

Vessel (*renmai*) in the front of the chest. The lower abdomen is involved, protruding during inhalation and contracting during exhalation. Proper use of breathing exercises can expand lung capacity. Scientific experiments have shown that lung capacity is directly proportional to strength and life expectancy. For example, individuals with deep, fine, even, and long breaths during sleep are generally robust, while those with short, weak, or irregular breaths are either ill or weak. The length and thickness of the breathing waves correspond to an individual's physical strength and vitality. Therefore, Tai Chi places significant emphasis on breathing in its fitness practice.

于睡眠状态呼吸深、细、匀、长的必是强健者，而呼吸短促无力或长、短不匀者非病即弱无疑。呼吸波的长短、粗细是一个人体质强弱配志。所以说，太极拳健身在呼吸上很是注重。

Ⅱ. Smooth *qi* and Blood Circulation, Promoting Blood Circulation

In Tai Chi practice, the aim is to extend *qi* (vital energy) to the extremities. The nourishment and moisturization of the body, from the external limbs, joints, muscles, and skin to the internal organs, vital energy, and spirit, are all dependent on the circulation of blood. A good blood circulation and sufficient blood supply are not only the fundamental guarantee for the normal functioning of various bodily functions but also the fundamental condition for determining the length of human life. Through the practice of Tai Chi's movements and postures, such as maintaining a vertical posture with the head suspended, sinking the energy to the *dantian* (lower abdomen), and

二、以意导气促进血液循环

太极拳锻炼要气达梢节。人体从外形的四肢八节，筋骨皮到内在的五脏六腑、精气神，都离不开血液的滋补润泽。良好的血液循环、充盈的血液供给，既是人体各部功能正常运行的基本保障，也是决定人体生命长短的根本条件。太极拳行功走架，竖项贯顶，虚灵顶劲，气沉丹田，以意导气，以气运身，内气上至百会、下通涌泉、达于四梢促进了血液循环，疏通了经络，加快了循环频率，大动脉畅通无阻，毛细血管经久不衰，四肢百骸，肌肤延缓了老化。长期坚持太极拳锻炼，则气血饱满、健康长寿。

guiding the *qi* with the mind, the internal energy is directed upwards to the *baihui* point, downwards to the *yongquan* point, and reaches out to the extremities, thereby promoting blood circulation, clearing the meridians, accelerating the circulation frequency of major arteries, ensuring unobstructed flow in capillaries, and delaying aging of the muscles, joints, and skin. Long-term adherence to Tai Chi practice results in abundant *qi* and blood, contributing to health and longevity.

Ⅲ. Smooth Sweat Glands, Ensuring Metabolism

三、汗腺通畅，保证新陈代谢

The waste generated by the human body's metabolism is eliminated through the seven orifices of the eyes, ears, nose, mouth, and the gastrointestinal tract. The main channel for endocrine secretion in the body is through the sweat glands. Additionally, sweat hairs and sweat pores have natural regulatory functions for temperature insulation and heat dissipation. Traditional Chinese medicine holds the saying, "When sweat glands are unobstructed, diseases do not invade; when sweat glands are blocked, various illnesses occur". In modern society, with the continuous improvement of material living conditions, centralized heating in winter and the availability of air conditioning and fans in summer have provided relief from extreme temperatures, but they have also led to a decrease in the skin's ability to keep warm and dissipate

人体新陈代谢所产生的废物除通过眼，耳、鼻、口七窍和谷道排泄外，机体内分泌主要是汗腺外排。除此汗毛与汗毛孔尚具有保温、散热的自然调节功能。因此中医有"汗腺通则百病不侵，汗腺堵则乱病缠身"一说。现代社会，人们的物质生活条件不断改善和提高，冬有集中供暖，夏有空调、电扇，免受寒暑之苦的同时，却又导致了人体皮肤保暖、散热功能的下降。由于汗毛变懒、汗毛孔堵塞、肌肤的通透性弱化，人体内脏分泌物、沉积物以及病毒等有害物质得不到及时排泄，新陈代谢失调，阴阳温热失衡，这样那样的疾病便会不染自生。而太极拳作为一门内家功法，在肌肤的锻炼上有其独到之处。行功走架不分春夏秋冬，拳架于身形的开合收放之中导引肌肤的膨缩和毛孔的张闭。练拳的人比一般不练拳的人较好地保持了肌肤的纯洁性和通透性，内分泌渠道畅通，病毒垃圾不易滞留，故而小病不生、大病不长。

heat. Due to decreased activity of sweat hairs, clogged sweat pores, and weakened skin permeability, harmful substances such as secretions, deposits, and viruses in the body are not promptly eliminated, resulting in metabolic imbalances and imbalances in Yin and Yang, leading to the onset of various diseases. However, Tai Chi, as an internal martial art, has unique aspects in terms of exercising the skin. The movements and postures in Tai Chi practice, regardless of the season, involve opening and closing, expanding and contracting of the body, which guides the expansion and contraction of the skin and opening and closing of the pores. Practitioners of Tai Chi maintain the purity and permeability of their skin better than those who do not practice, with unobstructed channels for endocrine secretion and reduced accumulation of viruses and waste materials. As a result, minor ailments are less likely to occur, and serious illnesses are less likely to develop.

Ⅳ. Symmetrical Movements, Compensating for Inherent Functional Insufficiency

四、对称运动，弥补人体机能后天不足

In daily life and work, people unconsciously develop various habitual patterns. While these habits enhance movement efficiency, they also lead to deficiencies in body movements. In other words, habitual movements are often unidirectional and biased. For example, in daily life, single-handed actions such as holding, grasping, lifting, and squeezing are usually performed

人们在日常生活、工作中有意无意地形成了诸多习惯定势。这些习惯定势一方面提高了动作效率，一方面也酿成了人体运动的缺陷。也就是说，凡是习惯动作多属单向偏颇运动。例如，日常生活中上肢的端、握、提、捏、抓等单手动作一般多用右手；下肢的弹、跳、蹦、踢等多以右足发力；中上盘的扛、挑、抬等多用右肩。左撇子者反之。无论是左还是右，均系单向运动。这种外形的单向运动，天长日久使大脑中枢神经减弱了

with the right hand, while lower limb actions such as bouncing, jumping, kicking, and exerting force are predominantly driven by the right foot. The same applies to the upper body, where actions such as carrying, lifting, and raising are predominantly executed with the right shoulder. The opposite applies to left-handed individuals. Regardless of left or right dominance, these are unidirectional movements. Prolonged engagement in such unidirectional movements weakens the brain's central nervous system's ability to regulate in the opposite direction, resulting in imbalances in internal bodily functions. When the right side is dominant, the left side becomes weaker, and vice versa. The strong side becomes thin, while the weak side becomes prone to illness. Hence, the common saying related to illness, "Men left, women right" . Although this statement may not be entirely scientific, it is commonly observed that diseases tend to cluster on one side of the body. The distinctive structure of Tai Chi forms a complete unity of "above and below" , with techniques alternating between left and right and the body's form complementing each other vertically. This creates symmetrical movements internally and externally. The emphasis on changing techniques and the sequence of movements in Tai Chi emphasizes starting with the left before the right and starting with the upper before the lower. When exerting force, it emphasizes front-outward expansion and rearward support, achieving a unified and integrated opposition of the whole body. As a result, the brain's ability for reverse

逆向调节功能,由此势必导致人体内部机能的左右失衡。右强则左弱左强则右弱。强者易瘦,弱者易病,故而在发病上有句"男左女右"的俗话。此说虽未必科学但人体患病多集于一侧确为常见。太极拳的造型结构恰恰是"有上即有下",招式左右互换、身形上下互补,形成内外如一的对称运动。抽招换式强调欲左先右、欲上先下;发力时讲求前吐后撑,周身上下对立统一、浑然一体。从而,有效地强化了大脑的逆向调节功能,保持了人体运动的整体协调与平衡发展,克服了单向运动致病的缺陷。

regulation is effectively strengthened, maintaining overall coordination and balanced development of bodily movements, overcoming the deficiencies caused by unidirectional movements that lead to illness.

V. Using Intention Rather Than Force, Enhancing Sensitivity of the Nervous System

五、用意不用力，提高神经系统的敏感度

Human body aging is characterized by the initial shrinking and deterioration of the nervous system. For instance, facial skin relaxation and wrinkles, forehead balding are caused by the decline in the regenerative function of nerve cells. Hearing loss, blurred vision result from the aging of auditory and visual nerves. Sluggish reactions and decreased memory are related to the aging of discriminating and retrieval nerves, while difficulty in leg movement is associated with the aging of central controlling nerves. All bodily functions are dependent on the functioning of hundreds of thousands of nerves. The atrophy of any single nerve directly leads to a decline in the function of a specific organ in the body. The significant difference between Tai Chi and other martial arts lies in its emphasis on using intention rather than force, focusing on the mind rather than the physical form, and using the mind to control the body's movements. In Tai Chi practice, complete attention is given to the mind, and the movements are guided by intention.

人体老化，神经系统最先萎缩和衰竭。例如：面部皮肤松弛起皱、前额脱发源于细胞再生神经的功能下降；耳聋眼花，源于听觉、视觉神经的老化；反应迟钝、记忆力下降源于分辨检索神经的老化。脚不利索源于中枢支配神经的老化。凡此种种，人体所有功能无不是源于十余万条神经的作用。任何一条神经的萎缩，都将直接导致人体某一器官功能的下降。太极拳与其他拳种的最大区别就在于它是一种用意不用力、重意不重形、以意念支配肉体的运动。太极拳行功走架，全神贯注，以意导气所有外形变化一招一式讲求意在身先，意不动身不动，意动身随，意静形止。

The so-called "intention" refers to various commands and signals issued by the

所谓意念，也即大脑中枢神经发出的各种指令和信号。太极拳每次行功走架首先

central nervous system in the brain. Every change in form and posture is based on the intention that precedes physical movement. Conversely, when practicing without a calm mind and focused intention, resulting in scattered thoughts and imbalanced internal and external coordination, the essence of Tai Chi as a movement is lost. Skilled Tai Chi practitioners, even in their old age, tend to maintain sharp hearing, clear vision, and nimble feet, and their skin sensitivity differs from that of ordinary individuals. The saying in martial arts that "not a feather can land, not a fly can perch" describes the heightened sensitivity of the skin of martial artists. All of these benefits are attributed to the practice of Tai Chi, which delays the aging of the nervous system by using intention in movement training.

是意运动,其次才是形体运动,也即人们常说的形神兼备。反之,练功心不静意不专形散意乱,内外失调,便失去了太极拳的运动本质。正是由于太极拳的这一功法特点,功深艺高的老拳师即使到了晚年,也多是耳不聋、眼不花、脚不沉,其肌肤的敏感性仍异于常人。拳论上所云"一羽不能加,蝇虫不能落",即是形容不丢不顶之意,也是概指拳手肌肤的灵敏度。所有这些,无不赖于用意练拳延缓了神经老化的缘故。

Ⅵ. Moderate Exercise Maintains the Homeostasis of Human Functions

六、运动适度,保持人体机能的中和态

Different opinions exist regarding the relationship between exercise and life. It is generally believed that life lies in movement, derived from the concept of flowing water that does not decay and a door hinge that does not get worm-eaten. Some people argue that life lies in being sedentary, aiming to reduce wear and tear on the body and the consumption of energy. Those who hold this view often compare it to the longevity of turtles and cranes. In reality, both perspectives have their merits, and the key lies in not neglecting either

就运动与生命的关系而言历来说法不一,通常认为:生命在于运动,其理取自流水不腐、户枢不蠹。也有人认为:生命在于多静,以减少机体的磨损和功能的消耗。持此观点者,多以龟龄鹤寿作比。实际上,这两种观点都有道理关键在于动与静不可偏废。生命在于运动不错,但超负荷的剧烈运动无疑会使机体疲劳早衰;而多静少动者,往往消化不良食欲不振,四肢乏力,精神萎靡病气易侵,故多长年不断药。所以说,过分地强调动或过分地主张静,均于人体健康不利,只有运动适度、动静相间的运动才有益于健康。太极拳行功走架进退往来为动,但用意不用拙力,消耗不大;就心境而言行

movement or stillness. Life indeed depends on movement, but excessive and intense exercise undoubtedly leads to early fatigue and aging of the body. On the other hand, individuals who are mostly sedentary often suffer from poor digestion, loss of appetite, weakness in limbs, mental decline, and are prone to illness, often relying on medication. Therefore, excessively emphasizing either movement or stillness is detrimental to human health. Only moderate exercise, alternating between movement and stillness, is beneficial to health. In Tai Chi practice, while performing movements and stances, there is an emphasis on relaxed and calm states. The term "stillness" here refers to abandoning distracting thoughts during the practice of movements or pushing hands, seeking a tranquil and focused state of mind where external forms may be in motion, yet the mind remains still. This unique way of practicing Tai Chi has a significant role in maintaining the homeostatic balance of human functions, which contributes to longevity through long-term practice.

功走架中强调放松入静。这里所说的"静"，是指走架或推手时须摒弃杂念，动中求静，神意专注，以一念代万念，所以说外形虽动心犹静。太极拳的这种独特运动方式对保持人体机能的中和平衡有很好的作用，故而久练可使人延年。

Ⅶ. Cultivating Long Breath and Flexibility, Preventing Aging of Bones, Joints, and Ligaments

Observing both the animal and plant kingdoms in nature, as well as the ecological development process of human beings themselves, it can be observed that vigorous living organisms possess good flexibility in their limbs or branches, while those nearing death become stiff and withered. In terms

七、长气致柔，防止骨质、关节、韧带的老化

无论是从自然界的动植物看，还是从人类自身的生态发展过程看，凡是生命力旺盛者，其肢体或肢干都具有良好的柔韧性；凡是行将死亡的有机体都会变得僵硬、枯萎。就人体而言，老年人骨质疏松发脆、关节旋转不灵、韧带松弛、血管干瘪等，无不是失去柔韧性的结果。欲使人体康壮不衰，就必须使周身筋骨皮保持良好的弹性。太极拳行

of the human body, conditions such as osteoporosis, joint stiffness, ligament laxity, and vascular atrophy in older individuals are all results of the loss of flexibility. To maintain a strong and resilient body, it is essential to keep the muscles, bones, and skin throughout the body elastic. In Tai Chi practice, movements such as finger rotations, wrist rotations, arm rotations, waist rotations, stretching tendons, and stretching bones are all performed in circular arcs. This spiral motion aims to enhance the flexibility, or in other words, the elasticity of muscles, bones, skin, and internal organs. Skilled practitioners of Tai Chi tend to have larger lung capacity, significant expansion and contraction of internal organs, long tendons and strong bones, supple skin, deep, smooth, and prolonged breaths, and larger angles of rotation in joints. These are all indications of good flexibility in the body. The extension of flexibility itself contributes to longevity, whereas the loss of elasticity in any organ within the human body signifies the end of life.

功走架，旋指、旋腕、旋膀、旋腰，撑裆开胯伸筋拔骨，缠绕拧翻所有招式动作，无不在画弧走圆中完成。这种螺旋运动的内涵，其实就在于强化周身筋、骨、皮及其内脏各器官的弹性亦即柔韧性。所以，功深艺高的太极拳手，多为肺活量大、脏腑胀缩差大、筋长骨坚、肌肤松软、呼吸深细匀长、关节正逆旋转角度大，这都是机体柔韧性良好的表现。柔韧性的延长本身就是长寿，反之人体内脏任何一个器官失去了弹性也就意味着生命的终结。

Ⅷ. Cultivating a Relaxed, Calm, Empty, and Tranquil State of Mind, Nurturing a Transcendent and Detached Mental State

八、松、静、空、灵，陶冶超然脱俗的心境

It is well known that individuals with a calm and contented mind tend to have longer lifespans, while those who follow an opposite path often perish prematurely. This is because individuals with excessive desires are constantly seeking, indulging in greed, excessive eating, worries, anxieties,

众所周知，清心寡欲的人多高寿，反其道而行者往往早亡。原因是多欲之人必多求，多求之人交贪饮、贪食、多忧、多虑、多思、多恼、多惊、多恐，凡欲有多必伤。中医认为哀伤神、怒伤肝、忧伤肺、思伤脾、虑伤心、恐伤肾、食多伤胃、房事多行伤精又伤气。太极拳的锻炼过程就是调节心性的过

excessive thoughts, agitation, and fear. It is believed in Chinese medicine that grief harms the spirit, anger harms the liver, worry harms the lungs, overthinking harms the spleen, excessive mental activity harms the heart, fear harms the kidneys, overeating harms the stomach, and excessive sexual activity depletes essence and energy. The practice of Tai Chi involves the process of regulating the state of mind. During the practice of movements and stances, every part of the body and mind should be relaxed, calm, empty, and tranquil. The key is to let actions flow naturally, without force, thus achieving a harmonious interaction between body and mind, resembling the fluidity of clouds and flowing water in the movements of advancing, retreating, and changing.

程。行功走架时,身心各部讲究松、静、空、灵,举手投足、身形变换贵在顺其自然,故而进退往来状如行云流水、身心俱佳。

第六节　太极拳的技击理论

Section 6: The Martial Arts Theory of Tai Chi

The effectiveness of Tai Chi in martial arts is extremely profound. While other forms of martial arts rely more or less on force to achieve victory, Tai Chi primarily emphasizes skill. Tai Chi practitioners are able to use their keen tactile sensitivity to redirect and avoid opposing forces, borrow and evade opponent's strength, and strike the opponent's vulnerabilities. Tai Chi employs

太极拳在技击上的效用极为奥妙,他种拳术或多或少要以力取胜,而太极拳则主要是以巧取胜。太极拳家能凭借皮肤敏锐的触觉,化人之力,借人之力,避实击虚,而操胜算。以太极拳应敌,主要靠"化"与"发",在每个圆圈形动作中,都包含着化守和发攻两个方面。而功夫越深,这个圆圈也就越小。

the principles of "transforming" and "issuing" during each circular movement, which encompass both defensive and offensive aspects. As one's skill deepens, the circular motion becomes smaller.

Tai Chi practitioners have the ability to nullify external forces, seize opportunities in the split second when the opponent attacks but has not yet returned or consolidated, and effectively use their internal power to unbalance the opponent, causing them to fall. The key lies in accurately assessing the timing. As stated in the *Da Shou Ge* (*Song of Pushing Hands*), it is crucial to "lead, redirect, press, and touch seriously, with upper and lower following each other, making it difficult for others to enter" . It further states, "When the opponent doesn't move, I don't move; when the opponent moves slightly, I move first. The power is like looseness but not looseness, it seems to be expanding but not expanding, the power breaks but the intention doesn't break." "It emphasizes the need to respond swiftly when the opponent moves quickly and to respond slowly when the opponent moves slowly." This illustrates how Tai Chi differs from martial arts that rely solely on brute force and physical confrontation. Tai Chi advocates letting go of oneself and adapting to the opponent, employing delayed action to achieve a preemptive advantage, and using intelligence and skill to overcome the enemy.

太极拳家能把外力引进使之落空,乘对方攻而未返、展而未收一刹那之间,乘虚运用发劲,使对方失去重心而倾跌,其关键全在于准确的审度时机。《打手歌》云:"掤捋挤按须认真,上下相随人难进"。又云:"彼不动,已不动;彼微动,已先动。劲似松非松,将展非展,劲断意不断";"动急则急应,动缓则缓随"。可见,太极拳与一切凭蛮力与敌拼搏之武术不同,主张舍已从人,后发先至,凭智与功力克敌。

Ⅰ. Principles of Tai Chi Martial Arts

Stillness Within Movement: The stillness in Tai Chi is the stillness within movement, encompassing both psychological and physiological aspects. Psychological stillness refers to remaining calm in the face of the opponent's ever-changing actions. Only with a calm mind can one discern the origin and trajectory of the opponent's force, allowing one to seize their vulnerabilities and launch a counterattack. In the dynamic and ever-changing circumstances of martial arts, one should always maintain stability in one's own center of gravity, which is the physiological stillness. While maintaining one's own stillness, one should strive to disrupt the opponent's mental and physical balance in order to facilitate one's own attacks. Waiting for the opponent to exhaust themselves and not wasting energy on unnecessary movements is the principle of stillness within movement.

Softness Overcomes Hardness: The technique of Tai Chi martial arts involves using softness that conforms to and stretches with the opponent's force, without opposing resistance. When faced with external force, one should avoid resisting and instead lead it to emptiness, causing it to fail. Then, one can expose the opponent's weaknesses and apply the principle of combined force to deliver a powerful strike, thus achieving the effect of overcoming hardness with softness and

一、太极拳技击原则

以静制动：太极拳之静，乃动中之静，包括心理与生理两方面。心理之静，指任敌千变万化，我只以镇静应之。惟心静才能辨明敌劲之来龙去脉，我才能乘其虚而攻之。在瞬息万变的技击情况下，我应始终保持自身重心的稳定，即生理之静。在保持自身静的同时，应千方百计地破坏对方心身的平衡，以利我之出击。以逸待劳，劲不虚发，即以静制动原则。

以柔克刚：太极拳技击系用随敌劲伸缩而不含抵抗之柔劲，它对任何加于我之力，抱定不抵抗态度，而是予以走化，使之落空，然后引出对方弱点，运用合力的原理发劲，从而收到以柔克刚以小胜大的技击效果。以柔克刚之理在于：刚劲是有限的，以刚应刚，则力弱者败；柔劲是无限的，敌力无论如何强大，我均以柔劲化之，则敌力于我何用？

winning against a stronger opponent. The principle of softness overcoming hardness lies in the fact that hardness has limitations. If one confronts hardness with hardness, the weaker party will be defeated. Softness, on the other hand, is limitless. No matter how strong the opponent's force is, it is rendered ineffective when met with softness.

Following the Principle of Yielding to Overcoming: The movements of Tai Chi Chuan consist of countless circles. The circular movements, through the technique of yielding to overcome, avoid any direct strikes from the opponent. When the force of the opponent's direct attack intersects with my circular motion, my rotation causes the force to disperse at an oblique angle, reducing its impact. The degree of retreat is directly proportional to the size of the oblique angle, resulting in efficient use of energy. I also use sticking and following techniques to trap the opponent within my circle, making their limbs feel entangled like being caught in a net, restricting their ability to advance or retreat. The mysteries of the circular movements in Tai Chi Chuan are infinite, but mastery is not easy. In the beginning, the movements may be large and clumsy, but with practice, they become smaller and more agile. Eventually, the intention of the circle is achieved without the visible form of a circle. By the time the opponent realizes my intention to strike, they have already fallen, as the transformation and execution occur in an instant.

以顺避逆：太极拳运动由无数圆圈组成，圆运动以逆来顺受技法避免了对手加于的直接打击。因直来之力与我之圆相交，我旋转使力成斜角而分散，减退之程度与斜角之大小成正比，故走化甚省力；我还用粘随把敌套入我之圆圈，使其手足如被网所缠缚，进退不得。太极拳之圆圈运动奥妙无穷，但得之非易。初练时大而笨，缠则小而活，终则有圈之意，无圈之形，出手尚未见其转圈，敌已跌出，盖化与发于刹那间已告完成。

Ⅱ. Steps of Tai Chi Quan Techniques

The specific implementation of Tai Chi Quan techniques involves four steps: "listening" (*ting*), "adhering" (*hua*), "seizing" (*na*), and "issuing" (*fa*). However, the primary goal is to achieve the state of "adhering, connecting, sticking, and following without losing the crown", which enables me to use the steps of listening, adhering, seizing, and issuing to control the opponent. Listening, adhering, seizing, and issuing are four fundamental internal energies among the various internal energies of Tai Chi Quan, and they are closely related to each other. Accurate listening to the opponent's energy allows for appropriate transformation of the opponent's energy. By grasping the focal point of the opponent's energy, which is the moment of obtaining the advantageous position of "my compliance with the opponent's back", I can utilize issuing energy to make the opponent fall. The transformation energy follows an arc-shaped trajectory, while the issuing energy follows a straight-line trajectory. This results in efficient use of force and yields significant results, representing the decisive strategic aspect of Tai Chi techniques.

It can be seen that Tai Chi Quan excels in the strategy of striking after the opponent has made a move. When the opponent is not moving, I cannot determine their true intentions. In such cases, I use a feigned attack to draw out the opponent's energy,

二、太极拳技击步骤

太极拳技击之具体实施有听、化、拿、发四个步骤。但首要做到"粘连粘随不丢顶",我即可用听、化、拿、发以制敌。听、化、拿、发为太极拳多种内劲中的四种基本内劲,且有密切相互关系。听敌之劲准确,化敌之劲才能恰当;拿住敌劲之焦点,也就是取得"我顺人背"的机势之际,我运用发劲,可使敌立仆。化劲走弧线,发劲走直线,力省而功巨,是为太极技击之决胜战略。

可见,太极拳善于后发制人。敌不动,我无从知其虚实,我先用一虚招把敌劲引出,我即化之、发之。若我之化劲不能达到使敌处于背势之境地,则我继续运用引劲、化劲,直至使敌背势时才用发劲,而收全功。

which I then transform and issue. If my transformation energy is not able to put the opponent in a disadvantaged position, I continue to use the techniques of drawing and transforming energy until the opponent is in a disadvantaged position, and then I use issuing energy to achieve complete success.

Ⅲ. Understanding Tai Chi Quan's Internal Energy

三、太极拳内劲之认识

Tai Chi Quan emphasizes the avoidance of any clumsiness and instead focuses on utilizing internal energy. Internal energy, in this context, refers to the energy that is developed through the practice of Tai Chi, characterized by circular, endless, externally soft but internally firm, and elastic strength. This kind of energy "does not manifest externally but is accumulated internally", thus it is called internal energy. Tai Chi employs quick and imperceptible movements, where power is generated at the moment of striking, without any prior indication of force, and after striking, there is no residual force. It only manifests power during the moment of striking the opponent, which is as swift as lightning. The release of energy is instantaneous, and it requires minimal effort. Correct application of energy is the key to Tai Chi techniques. The main internal energies of Tai Chi Quan are described as follows:

太极拳强调丝毫不用拙力,着重运用内劲。所谓内劲,就是在练拳中得到的环而无端,周而复始,外柔内刚且富有弹性的劲,这种劲“形不外露,功蕴于内”,故称内劲。太极用劲,灵捷无形,手到发劲,未中之先无劲,既中之后无劲,只在中敌之刹那发劲,疾如闪电,一发传收,敛气凝神,毫不费力。正确用劲为太极技击关键。兹将太极拳主要内劲分述如下:

Adhering and Sticking Energy: This refers to the energy that does not lose contact with the opponent. Adhering and sticking

沾粘劲:即不丢之劲。沾粘即粘贴之意,把敌粘住之劲。敌进我退,敌退我进,敌浮我随,敌沉我松。初练推手时,手臂知觉

mean to stick and attach to the opponent's energy. When the opponent advances, I retreat; when the opponent retreats, I advance; when the opponent floats, I follow; when the opponent sinks, I loosen. In the initial practice of pushing hands, the arms lack sensitivity and feel like wooden sticks. However, with continuous practice, the sensitivity gradually improves, starting from the arms, extending to the shoulders, chest, and back, and eventually reaching the whole body, including the skin. Only with this sensitivity can one adhere and stick. With adherence and sticking energy, the opponent can be effectively captured. Adhering and sticking energy is the first step in the introductory stage, and without this energy, it is difficult to delve into other internal energies.

不灵,犹如木棍,日久感觉渐趋灵敏,由手臂而肩而胸而背,乃至周身皮肤,逐渐生有感觉。有感觉始可沾粘。有沾粘,始可将敌吸住。沾粘劲为入门初步,此劲不通,难以深入其他之内劲。

Listening Energy: The term "listening" in Tai Chi Quan does not refer to using the ears but rather using the sense of touch through the skin to perceive the opponent's energy. Therefore, it is crucial to first master adhering and sticking energy to firmly capture the opponent. With adhering and sticking, one can listen accurately and understand the changes in the opponent's energy. The key to listening energy lies in relaxing the waist and legs, gathering one's energy, and achieving a state of relaxation, softness, sinking, stillness, and stability. Without these qualities, it is challenging to accurately listen to the opponent's energy.

听劲:所谓听,并非用耳,而以皮肤之触觉去感知敌劲。故必先掌握沾粘劲将敌紧紧吸住。能沾粘,才能听;能听,才能懂敌劲之变化。听劲之关键在于松腰腿,敛气凝神,做到松、柔、沉、静、稳,否则无从准确听敌之劲。

Transforming Energy: Transforming energy in Tai Chi Quan involves both adhering and sticking energy and ward-off energy (*bing jin*). Without these two energies, transformation cannot occur. The focus of transformation lies in the waist and not in the hands or shoulders. If the transformation is done forcefully without utilizing the principles of Tai Chi, it becomes a rigid push rather than the genuine transformation energy of Tai Chi Quan. The key point is to follow the opponent's back and employ folding, returning, and changing movements to put the opponent in a disadvantaged position. Energy should not be completely transformed; otherwise, the adhering and sticking energy will easily break, and the momentum will be lost. It is important to time the transformation neither too early nor too late. The most opportune moment to apply transformation energy is when the opponent's energy is about to be released but has not fully manifested or when the opponent's energy is about to arrive but has not fully arrived. With proper timing, the transformation energy can be effective.

化劲：化劲中须含沾粘劲和掤劲，否则不能化。机枢在腰而不在手、肩，否则是谓硬拨，非真太极拳之化劲也。其要点全我顺人背，须有往复褶迭和进退转换，使敌无由知我劲路，从而达到使对方处于背势的境地。劲不可化尽，化尽则我之沾粘劲易断，而去势随之远矣。又不可过早或过迟，太早未到，无有所化；过迟则敌劲已着，化之无益。运用化劲最恰当的时机是敌劲将出而未全出、将至而未全至之际。化之得势，发之才有效。

Issuing Energy: Issuing energy refers to the internal energy used to strike the opponent in Tai Chi techniques. When practicing issuing energy, it is essential to understand the path of energy. Issuing energy requires controlling the opponent's "root" . The entire body of a person can be seen as a tree, with the feet as the root, the torso as the branches, and the head as the leaves. In the upper body, the shoulders are

发劲：为太极技击中攻敌之内劲。习发劲之初，当先知劲路。发劲须制敌之"根"。人之全身，足为根，身为枝，头为叶；人之上身，肩为根，肘为枝，手为叶；人之下身，腿为根，膝为枝，足为叶。拿人发人，先制其根，是取胜的关键。能明此旨，方可发人。

the root, the elbows are the branches, and the hands are the leaves. In the lower body, the legs are the root, the knees are the branches, and the feet are the leaves. To control the opponent, it is crucial to first control their root. Understanding this principle allows for effective issuing of energy.

Issuing energy must fulfill three essential aspects: ① Timing and momentum, ② Direction, and ③ Timing. All three are indispensable. Timing and momentum involve aligning one's own momentum with the opponent's back when their center of gravity is shifting. Direction can be up or down, left or right, or straight, depending on the opponent's back. Timing refers to the moment when the opponent's old energy has dissipated, and new energy has not yet fully emerged. When all three aspects are present, issuing energy becomes effortless, like releasing a projectile with favorable results. When issuing energy, the body should be aligned, the waist should be relaxed, the legs should be rooted, the shoulders should sink, and the energy should be connected throughout the limbs. The focus should be on the opponent, without any doubt or hesitation, with the intention to strike effectively. This represents the profound essence of issuing energy in Tai Chi Quan.

发劲必须达到三要点：①机势；②方向；③时间。三者不可缺一，机势，即己势顺敌势背，在对方重心偏离之际。方向，或上或下，或左或右，或正或隅，均须随敌之背而发之。时间，即在敌旧劲已完，新劲未生之时，为最确当。三者俱全，则发人甚易。犹如弹丸脱手，无往不利。发劲时己身应尾闾中正，坐腰松胯，虚领顶劲，沉肩坠肘，气贴脊背，而贯之于肢体，目注对方，勿存疑虑之心，意欲发之于远。此方得太极发劲之妙谛。

Lifting Energy: Lifting energy refers to the upward lifting force used to disrupt the opponent's root and make their center of gravity tilt. The method of lifting energy primarily relies on the waist and legs, not the hands. Lifting with the hands makes

提劲：提即上提拔高之劲，用沾粘劲拔敌之根，使其重心倾斜。提的方法全在腰腿，非用手提，手提则重而笨，易被人发觉。提时桩步须稳，丹田气松，虚领顶劲，敛气凝神，用腰腿劲向上沾提，方向、距离、身法、步法，处处与对方凑合，方能奏效。

the movement heavy and clumsy, making it easier for the opponent to detect. When lifting, the stance should be stable, the lower abdomen should be relaxed, the crown of the head should be suspended, and the energy should be gathered in the waist and legs. The direction, distance, body posture, and footwork should all be coordinated with the opponent for the technique to be effective.

Ward-Off Energy: Ward-off energy (*bing jin*) is crucial in push hands exercises. When applying ward-off energy, the forearms should maintain a certain distance from the chest, and as one's skill deepens, this distance becomes smaller. Whether rotating to the left or right, advancing or retreating, this energy should not be neglected. By utilizing the power of the waist and legs, coordinating with leading energy and transforming energy, the forearms rotate and roll, redirecting the opponent's force diagonally and preventing it from penetrating.

掤劲：掤劲在推手中甚为重要，运用时前臂与胸部须保持一定距离，功夫越深，距离越小。无论左旋右转，前进后退，此劲均不可丢。运用腰腿劲，配合引劲、化劲，前臂旋转滚动，使敌力转向斜方而不能攻入。

Rolling Back Energy: Rolling back energy is based on ward-off energy and involves redirecting the opponent's energy backward, causing their center of gravity to shift towards the practitioner. The key lies in the twisting and sitting of the waist and hips, which drives the sinking of the shoulders and the pulling back of the arms towards the rear. Rolling back includes lifting and sinking aspects, with the waist rotating in accordance with the direction of the opponent's energy. Only then can the opponent be made to lean forward or move

捋劲：是在掤劲基础上将敌劲后引，使敌重心偏离，扑向我身之后方。劲源主要在于腰胯地拧坐，带动两肩下沉，扣劲转体，催动两臂向后方引带。捋中有提，捋中有沉，转动腰部，顺应敌劲方向，方能得心应手。不能捋，既不能使对方前俯，更不能移动其重心。重心不动，取胜难矣。

their center of gravity. Without the ability to roll back, it is impossible to make the opponent lean forward, let alone move their center of gravity. Without moving the center of gravity, it becomes challenging to achieve victory.

Squeezing Energy: Squeezing energy involves using the forearm to press against the opponent's body. The power for squeezing energy comes from the waist and legs. When squeezing, the rear leg generates a thrusting force, the front leg has a bowing force, the waist has a thrusting and lengthening force. With these forces, the arms are propelled forward, creating a pressing force.

挤劲：以前臂挤击人身，其劲力产生于腰腿。挤时，后腿有蹬劲，前腿有弓劲，腰有挺劲、长劲。由此催动两臂向前产生推压之劲。

Pressing Energy: Pressing energy is applied by pressing or striking the opponent's body or limbs with one or both hands. To gain an advantageous position, one must align with the opponent's movements and relax the waist, sink the hips, suspend the crown of the head, and avoid leaning the upper body forward, as this would shift the center of gravity forward and make it easier for the opponent to redirect the energy. Pressing energy can involve long energy, intercepting energy, sinking energy, and more, which can be used as appropriate in different situations.

按劲：按以单手或双手按击人身或连臂带人按发。按以顺步为得势，须坐腰松胯，虚领顶劲，沉肩坠肘，上身勿前俯，俯则重心向前，易被化引。按发中分有长劲、截劲、沉劲等，可随机而施。

Plucking Energy: Plucking energy involves grasping the opponent's wrist or elbow and pulling downward. The power for plucking energy mainly comes from twisting energy in the waist, sitting energy and

采劲：即以手执人手腕或肘部，往下沉采。其劲力主要来源于腰的拧劲，胯的坐劲、裹劲，腿的剪劲，脚掌的抓劲。运用这些劲力催动两肩，带动两臂随转体向下沉采。

wrapping energy in the hips, shearing energy in the legs, and grabbing energy in the soles of the feet. By utilizing these energy forces, the shoulders are mobilized, and the arms follow the rotation of the body, pulling downward.

Splitting Energy: Splitting energy mainly generates a horizontal force. Whether it is a left or right split, it relies on the twisting and sitting energy in the waist and hips, as well as the gripping energy in the legs, to drive the arms in a horizontal splitting motion.

挒劲：挒劲主要是一个横向的劲力。不管是左挒或右挒，全靠腰胯的拧坐劲、塌劲，两脚的扣劲，带动两臂向左右横挒。

Elbow Energy: Elbow energy is a penetrating force that works in conjunction with the knees. By employing the power of the waist and legs, and combining it with focused intention, the body remains upright, the crown of the head is suspended, the chest is hollow, the shoulders sink, and the tailbone is tucked. The rear leg generates a forward thrust, and the front leg has a bowing force. The eyes are focused on the opponent.

肘劲：此乃钻心之劲，应与膝相合，用腰腿劲加以意气，己身正直，虚领顶劲，含胸拔背，松肩沉肘，尾闾收住，后脚有前蹬劲，前腿有弓劲，眼神注视对方。

Bumping Energy: Bumping energy refers to using the shoulder to strike the opponent's chest. Once the bump connects with the opponent, a shaking force is released. When bumping, the body should be aligned and the shoulder and hips should be connected, avoiding forcefully colliding with the opponent's body using the shoulder. The power mainly comes from the rear leg's thrust, the waist's thrust, and the driving force of the back and shoulders. When bumping, the body should emit a sudden and rapid shaking force.

靠劲：一般指以肩靠击人之胸部。一旦靠贴住对方，即用抖劲发放。靠时己身中正，肩与胯合，不可以肩硬撞敌身。其劲力主要有后腿的蹬劲，腰的挺劲，催动背、肩靠击对方。靠击时要求身体发出快速突然的抖劲。

1–1

第二章　太极拳基本功

Chapter 2: Fundamental Skills of Tai Chi Quan

第一节　基本手型

Section 1: Basic Hand Forms

Ⅰ. Palm

The five fingers naturally extend, with the palm slightly facing forward (Figure 2-1).

一、掌

五指自然伸展,掌心微向前撑(图 2-1)。

Ⅱ. Fist

The four fingers curl inward, with the thumb pressing against the middle joint of the index and middle fingers. The fist is held relaxed yet containing internal power (Figure 2-2).

二、拳(捶)

四指内卷,拇指压在食指、中指的中节,握拳舒松而内含力量(图 2-2)。

Ⅲ. Hook

The wrist is bent, and the first joint of the five fingers is clenched(Figure 2-3).

三、勾

屈腕,五指第一指节捏拢(图 2-3)。

图 2-1 掌

图 2-2 拳

图 2-3 勾

第二节 基本步型

Section 2: Basic Footwork

Ⅰ. Bow Stance

Stand with one foot in front and the other foot behind. The front leg is bent, with the lower leg perpendicular to the ground. Push back with the rear leg without fully extending it. The feet should maintain an appropriate width, not in a straight line (Figure 2-4).

一、弓步

两脚前后开立，前腿屈，小腿与地面垂直，后腿舒展蹬地，不可绷直。左右脚保持适当宽度，不可前后一条线上(图 2-4)。

Ⅱ. Horse Stance

Relax the waist, tuck in the buttocks, and sink the hips. The center of gravity is biased toward the rear leg (Figure 2-5).

二、马步

松腰、敛臀、落胯，重心落于两脚之间(图 2-5)。

Ⅲ. Empty Stance

Relax the waist, tuck in the buttocks, and sink the hips. The center of gravity is supported by the rear leg, and the front foot's toe or heel lightly touches the ground (Figure 2-6).

三、虚步

松腰、敛臀、落胯，重心靠后腿支撑，前脚脚尖或脚跟虚点地面(图 2-6)。

Ⅳ. Crouch Stance

Spread the legs apart, with one leg fully squatting and the other leg extended straight and flat on the ground with the entire foot touching the floor (Figure 2-7).

四、仆步

两腿左右分开，一腿屈膝全蹲，另一腿伸直平仆，两脚全脚掌着地(图 2-7)。

Ⅴ. Cross Stance

Straighten the chest, lift the waist, and cross the legs with both knees bent. The front foot is fully planted on the ground with the toes pointing outward, while the heel of the rear foot is lifted, and the outer side of the hip is pressed against the lower leg (Figure 2-8).

五、歇步

挺胸、立腰，两腿交叉屈膝全蹲，前脚全掌着地，脚尖外展；后脚跟离地，臀部外侧紧贴后小腿(图 2-8)。

图 2-4 弓步

图 2-5 马步

图 2-6 虚步

图 2-7 仆步

图 2-8 歇步

Insights on Techniques: Traditional Chinese martial arts have accompanied the development of Chinese history and civilization for thousands of years. They have become the soul that sustains the survival and development of this nation, and the essence that carries the genetic makeup of the Chinese people, representing a treasure of the Chinese nation. Tai Chi, as an important component of Chinese martial arts, is a precious treasure that has been accumulated and preserved throughout the generations. Its theoretical foundation stems from ancient Chinese philosophical thoughts, presenting concepts of harmonious coexistence of *yin* and *yang*, the blending of softness and hardness, and the principle of overcoming hardness with softness. It emphasizes the unity of nature and humanity, as well as the interrelationship between human beings and nature, reflecting the profound and continuous spiritual connotation of Chinese traditional culture.

招式感悟：中国传统武术伴随着中国历史与文明发展，走过了几千年的风雨历程，成为维系这个民族生存和发展的魂和承载中华儿女基因构成的魄，是中华民族的瑰宝。太极拳作为中国武术的重要组成，是历代沉淀而成、安魂定魄的法宝。太极拳的理论基础来自中国古老的哲学思想，呈现了阴阳和谐相处、柔中带刚、以柔克刚等思想，强调的是天人合一、人与自然的相互关系，反映了中国传统文化的深刻、绵延不绝的精神内涵。

By practicing Tai Chi, we elevate ourselves from the body to the mind, from the soul to the essence, gaining a sense of security and empowerment. It strengthens our spirit, energizes our body, and bestows us with the ability to overcome challenges with calmness and self-assurance. The purpose of the Tai Chi philosophy is to explain nature, regulate society, and hope that people, based on their understanding of the cosmic principles of transformation and generation, consciously conform to the natural laws of Tai Chi in their activities. This includes the communication between heaven and humanity, the correspondence between heaven and humanity, and the unity of heaven and humanity. It emphasizes the unity of self and the external world, the transformation of external and internal, ultimately leading to a harmonious state of acceptance and tranquility, where all things find their rightful place.

我们修习太极拳,是让我们从身到心、由魂而魄得到提升而充满安全感,精壮神足,具有安然自胜的实力。太极理念的目的是用来解释自然、规范社会,并希望人们在认识宇宙万物化生大道的基础上,人类活动自觉顺应太极自然法则,天人相通、天人相应、天人合一,物我同体,顺外化内,最终到达一种无所不容、万物咸宁的和谐状态。

2-1

第三章　太极拳规范动作、劲法、呼吸、实战技法

Chapter 3: Tai Chi Form, Techniques, Breathing, and Practical Combat Skills

第一节　起势、左右野马分鬃、白鹤亮翅

Section 1: Opening Movement, Wild Horse's Mane, White Crane Spreads Its Wings

Preparatory Stance: Stand with feet together (Figure 3-1).

预备式：并步直立(图 3-1)。

Key Points of the Movements: Maintain a calm mind and relaxed body, keep the head upright and suspended, sink the energy to the *dantian*, and root the energy in the feet. Maintain a balanced and centered posture.

动作要领：心静体松，头虚领，气沉丹田劲沉脚，中正不偏。

图 3–1

Ⅰ. Opening Movement

1.Movement Explanation

(1) Slightly bend the knees, shift the weight to the right side, lift the left foot and take a step to the side, aligning with shoulder width or slightly wider, with the toes touching the ground first and then fully planting the foot (Figure 3-2 to 3-4).

(2) Bend the knees slightly, lift the hands up as the body rises, with the upper arms and forearms raised in front of the body, aligned with shoulder level, palms facing downward, and wrists relaxed (Figure 3-5 and 3-6).

(3) Squat down, lower the elbows, and press them down to the front of the abdomen (Figure 3-7 to 3-9).

Figure 3-2 to 3-4: Feet opening stance

Figure 3-5 and 3-6: Arms raising in front

Figure 3-7 to 3-9: Squatting and pressing palms

一、起势

(一)动作图解

(1)膝微屈,重心右移,提左脚外开一步,与肩宽齐宽或略宽于肩,脚尖先着地后至全脚掌着地(图 3-2—3-4)。

(2)膝微屈,起身提手,大臂带小臂两臂前举,与肩齐平,掌心向下,手腕放松(图 3-5、3-6)。

(3)两腿屈蹲,落肘下按至腹前(图 3-7—3-9)。

图 3-2—3-4 两脚开立
图 3-5、3-6 两臂前举
图 3-7—3-9 屈膝按掌

图 3–2

图 3–3

图 3–4

图 3–5

图 3–6

图 3–7

图 3–8

图 3–9

2. Breathing Method

（二）呼吸方法

Inhale while raising the foot, exhale while placing the foot down; inhale while raising the hands forward, exhale while squatting down and pressing the palms.

提脚吸气，落脚呼气，提手前举吸气，下蹲按掌呼气。

3. Analysis of Power Pathway

（三）劲路解析

Relax both arms and utilize the force generated by leg extension and waist elevation to lift the arms upward. Sink the energy and lower the hips to facilitate downward pressing of both hands.

两臂放松，利用蹬腿拔腰的力量带动手臂上举；沉气、落胯，利用身体的沉劲，促使两手下按。

4. Examples of Practical Application

（四）实战应用举例

Scenario 1: Party B embraces Party A from behind; Party A lowers the center of gravity, extends the arms outward, simultaneously turns and strikes with the elbow, hitting the abdomen of Party B (Figure 3-10 to 3-13).

场景 1：乙方从后方抱住甲方；甲方下蹲重心、手臂向外撑开，同时转身、击肘，击打乙方腹部（图 3-10—3-13）。

Scenario 2: Party B grabs the arm of Party A and attempts to perform a back throw; Party A slightly bends the knees, lowers the center of gravity, simultaneously pulls the hands backward and downward, causing Party B to fall to the ground (Figure 3-14 to 3-17).

场景 2：乙方拉住甲方手臂进行背摔；甲方微微屈膝下蹲，同时双手向后回收并且下拉，使乙方落空倒地（图 3-14—3-17）。

图 3–10

图 3–11

图 3–12

图 3–13

图 3–14

图 3–15

图 3–16

图 3–17

5. Insights on Styles

（五）招式感悟

The rise and fall, like the surging tide, the pull and empty, a limitless art. The "Opening Movement" may seem simple and even overlooked at times, yet it encompasses the essence of Tai Chi. Just as with the movements, this principle applies to how we approach life and tasks,

一起一落，似潮头汹涌，一引一空，妙法无穷，表面简单实则不简单。"起势"动作看似简单，甚至有时被忽略，但却包含了太极的全部精髓。动作如此，做人做事亦是如此，要求我们想问题、办事情都要以具体的时间、地点和条件为转移。很多时候我们要化繁为简，剖去烦冗，摒弃一切杂念，守住核心，正所谓"大道至简"。

requiring us to consider specific time, place, and conditions. Often, we need to simplify, eliminate complexity, abandon all distracting thoughts, and hold onto the core, as the saying goes, "The greatest simplicity is found in the ultimate truth."

Ⅱ. Left and Right Wild Horse's Mane

二、左右野马分鬃

1.Movement Explanation

(一)动作图解

(1) Shift the weight to the right side, lift the left foot and touch the ground; the right hand arcs upward, the left hand turns the palm downward and lowers, bringing the palms together in front of the body; the right hand is at chest level, the left hand is at the lower abdomen (Figure 3-18 to 3-21).

(1)重心右移,收左脚点地;右手画弧上行,左手翻掌下落,两掌心相对合抱于体前;右手在胸口高度,左手在小腹高度(图3-18—3-21)。

(2) Slightly turn the body to the left, step out to the left side with the left foot, touching the heel to the ground first (Figure 3-22).

(2)身体微左转,左脚左侧出步,脚跟先着地(图3-22)。

(3) Push off with the right leg and rotate the waist, the left foot forms a stable bow stance; the left arm extends forward and outward with the palm slanting upward, the right hand extends backward and downward with the palm facing downward, tiger's mouth facing forward, both hands spread apart (Figure 3-23 to 3-26).

(3)蹬右腿转腰,左脚踏实成弓步;左手臂向前、向外手掌斜向上,右手向后、向下,手掌向下,虎口朝前,两手分掌展开(图3-23—3-26)。

Figure 3-18 to 3-21：Collecting the foot and holding the ball

Figure 3-22：Left turn and step out

Figure 3-23 to 3-26：Bow stance and separating hands

（4）Shift the weight backward into a rear-leaning stance, relax both arms, and turn the right foot outward（Figure 3-27）.

（5）Shift the weight forward, place the right foot down；the left hand arcs upward, the right hand turns the palm downward and joins the left hand, palms facing each other in front of the body（Figure 3-28）.

（6）Slightly turn the body to the right, step out to the right side with the right foot, touching the heel to the ground first（Figure 3-29）.

（7）Push off with the left leg and rotate the waist, the right foot forms a stable bow stance；the right arm extends forward and outward with the palm slanting upward, the left hand extends backward and downward with the palm facing downward, tiger's mouth facing forward, both hands spread apart（Figure 3-30 and 3-31）.

Figure 3-27：Rear-leaning stance

Figure 3-28：Collecting the foot and holding the ball

Figure 3-29：Right turn and step out

Figure 3-30 and 3-31：Bow stance and separating hands

图 3-18—3-21 收脚抱球

图 3-22 左转出步

图 3-23—3-26 弓步分手

（4）重心后移成后坐步，两手臂放松，左脚尖外撇（图 3-27）。

（5）重心前移，收右脚点地；左手画弧上行，右手翻掌与左手合抱球与体前，掌心相对（图 3-28）。

（6）身体微右转，右脚右侧出步，脚跟先着地（图 3-29）。

（7）蹬左腿转腰，右脚踏实成弓步；右手臂向前、向外手掌斜向上，左手向后、向下手掌向下，虎口朝前，两手分掌展开（图 3-30、3-31）。

图 3-27 后坐步

图 3-28 收右脚抱球

图 3-29 右转出步

图 3-30、3-31 弓步分掌

(8) Shift the weight backward into a rear-leaning stance, relax both arms, and turn the nght foot outward (Figure 3-32).

(9) Shift the weight forward, place the left foot down; the right hand arcs upward, the left hand turns the palm downward and joins the right hand, palms facing each other in front of the body (Figure 3-33 and 3-34).

(10) Slightly turn the body to the left, step out to the left side with the left foot, touching the heel to the ground first (Figure 3-35).

(11) Push off with the right leg and rotate the waist, the left foot forms a stable bow stance; the left arm extends forward and outward with the palm slanting upward, the right hand extends backward and downward with the palm facing downward, tiger's mouth facing forward, both hands spread apart (Figure 3-35 and 3-37).

Figure 3-32: Rear-leaning stance

Figure 3-33 and 3-34: retracting the foot and holding the ball

Figure 3-35: Left turn and step out

Figure 3-36 and 3-37: Bow stance and separating hands

(8)重心后移成后坐步,两手臂放松,右脚尖外撇(图 3-32)。

(9)重心前移,收左脚点地;右手画弧上行,左手翻掌与右手合抱球与体前,掌心相对(图 3-33、3-34)。

(10)身体微左转,左脚左侧出步,脚跟先着地(图 3-35)。

(11)蹬右腿转腰,左脚踏实成弓步;左手臂向前、向外手掌斜向上,右手向后、向下手掌向下,虎口朝前,两手分掌展开(图 3-36、3-37)。

图 3-32 后坐步

图 3-33、3-34 收左脚抱球

图 3-35 左转出步

图 3-36、3-37 弓步分掌

图 3–18

图 3–19

图 3–20

图 3–21

图 3–22

图 3–23

图 3–24

图 3–25

图 3–26

图 3–27

图 3–28

图 3–29

图 3–30

图 3–31

图 3–32

图 3–33

图 3–34

图 3–35

图 3–36

图 3–37

2. Breathing Method

Starting from the initial position, shift the weight to the right, lift the left foot and inhale; place the left foot on the ground and exhale while embracing the ball; inhale while stepping forward on the left side, exhale while performing the bow stance and separating the palms. Shift the weight backward and inhale; embrace the ball with the trailing foot and exhale; inhale while stepping forward on the right side, exhale while performing the bow stance and separating the palms; shift the weight backward and inhale; embrace the ball with the trailing foot and exhale; inhale while stepping forward on the left side, exhale while performing the bow stance and separating the palms.

(二)呼吸方法

接起势,右移重心提左脚吸气,左脚点地抱球呼气,左侧上步吸气,弓步分掌呼气;后移重心吸气,跟步抱球呼气,右侧上步吸气,弓步分掌呼气;后移重心吸气,跟步抱球呼气,左侧上步吸气,弓步分掌呼气。

3. Analysis of Power Pathway

During practice, after stepping forward, generate force by pushing off with the rear leg, utilizing the force from the leg, waist, torso, and hands. When pushing off with the leg and rotating the waist, it is important to fully experience the power of the waist and groin area. When separating the palms, the forearms should have a twisting power. The “wild horse separates its mane” emphasizes the “leverage power”, which is a lateral power that has the effect of intercepting and cutting off the opponent’s waist. In actual combat applications, it can

(三)劲路解析

演练时,上步后,后腿蹬地要力,力由腿及腰及躯干及手,蹬腿转腰时,要充分体会腰裆劲,分掌时前臂要有拧劲。“野马分鬃”主打“挒劲”,挒劲为横向劲,有拦腰截断之势。实际对抗运用时可配合向下落空、向前发放等演示出更多的发放方向。

be combined with downward deflection and forward issuing to demonstrate more issuing directions.

4. Examples of Practical Application

（四）实战应用举例

Party B pushes Party A from the front using both hands. Party A grabs Party B's arm with the left hand, steps forward with the left leg, pulls down Party B's arm with the left hand, presses against Party B's left armpit with the right hand, steps forward with the right foot behind Party B's left leg, locks Party B's leg with the knee joint, pushes off the ground, rotates the waist, and uses force from the waist to knock the opponent down to the right side (Figure 3-38 to 3-42).

乙方从正面用双手推甲方；甲方左手抓住乙方手臂、左腿上步靠近，左手向下按拉乙方手臂，右手贴靠乙方左侧腋下，右脚上步到乙方左腿的后方，膝关节扣住乙方腿部，蹬地旋转、腰部发力，把对方向右侧击倒（图 3-38—3-42）。

图 3-38

图 3-39

图 3-40

图 3-41

图 3-42

5. Insights on Styles

（五）招式感悟

The movement of the material world is absolute, yet within its motion, there is a certain relative stillness. The absoluteness of motion embodies the variability and unconditionality of material motion, while the relativity of stillness embodies the stability and conditionality of material motion. Motion and stillness depend on each

物质世界的运动是绝对的，而物质在运动过程中又有某种相对的静止。运动的绝对性体现了物质运动的变动性、无条件性，静止的相对性体现了物质运动的稳定性、有条件性。运动和静止相互依赖、相互渗透、相互包含，"动中有静、静中有动"。避实就虚，你横我纵，你纵我横，不要以力硬碰力，换个方向也许就巧妙无穷。生活中亦是如

other, permeate each other, and contain each other. "In motion, there is stillness; in stillness, there is motion." Avoid the real and take the virtual, with horizontal and vertical movements. Don't collide force against force, as a change in direction may lead to ingenious possibilities. This also applies to life—maintain a humble attitude and avoid forcing things; by changing perspectives, new opportunities may be discovered. As the saying goes, "Be still as a virgin, move like a hare, silent yet astonishing."

此,要保持谦虚的态度,凡事不要硬来,换个角度看事物也许会发现新的契机。正所谓"静若处子,动若脱兔,不鸣则已,一鸣惊人"。

Ⅲ. Spreading Wings Like a White Crane

三、白鹤亮翅

1. Movement Demonstration

(一)动作图解

(1) From the previous position, shift the weight forward, and the right foot takes a half step forward. Both hands turn the palms and embrace the ball in front of the body (Figure 3-43 and 3-44).

(2) The right foot touches the ground firmly, the body slightly turns to the right, the right arm lifts up, and the left hand follows. The left foot lifts up without bearing weight (Figure 3-45 to 3-47).

(3) The left foot extends forward with the toes touching the ground, forming an empty step. The body slightly turns to the left, sitting upright. The right hand rises upward, while the left hand arcs down and presses, forming an empty step with the palm extension (Figure 3-48 and 3-49).

(1)接上式,重心前移,右脚往前跟半步,两手翻掌体前抱球(图 3-43、3-44)。

(2)右脚着地落实,身体微右转,右臂上提左手跟随,左脚放虚拎起(图 3-45—3-47)。

(3)左脚前伸脚尖着地成虚步,身体微左转坐正,右手上引,左手画弧下按,成虚步托掌(图 3-48、3-49)。

Figure 3-43, 3-44: Embrace the Ball with a Follow Step

Figure 3-45—3-47: Sit Back and Raise Arms

Figure 3-48, 3-49: Empty Step and Palm Extension

图 3-43、3-44 跟步抱球

图 3-45—3-47 后坐举臂

图 3-48、3-49 虚步分掌

图 3–43

图 3–44

图 3–45

图 3–46

图 3–47

图 3–48

图 3–49

2. Breathing Method

(二)呼吸方法

From the previous position, shift the weight forward and inhale. Exhale as the foot lands with a follow step. Inhale while lifting the upper arm, and exhale with the empty step and palm separation.

接上式，重心前移吸气，跟步落实呼气，右上举臂吸气，虚步分掌呼气。

3. Analysis of Power Pathway

(三)劲路解析

Clear distinction between the empty and solid footwork is necessary. The force starts from the feet, distributed to the waist and spine, and extends to the arms. Therefore, when performing the palm separation, one should pay attention to the rotational effect of the torso. The Baihe Liangchi technique emphasizes the rotation and opening movement, highlighting the importance of the central axis of the body during its application.

腿上虚实转换要分明,力由脚起,分配于腰脊,达于手臂,故分掌时要体会躯干的旋转作用。白鹤亮翅走偏劲,有开门旋转之意,运用时要注重躯干的中轴作用。

4. Examples of Practical Application

(四)实战应用举例

Scenario 1: Party B uses the right arm to push Party A's torso from the front. Party A's left hand holds Party B's wrist, while the right hand attaches to Party B's elbow joint, performing a lifting motion toward the upper-right direction, causing Party B to be thrown to the right side (Figure 3-50 to 3-54).

场景1:乙方用右臂从正面推甲方躯干,甲方左手按住乙方手腕,右手从下向上贴靠乙方肘关节,并向右后上方做提挑动作,将乙方向右侧甩出(图3-50—3-54)。

Scenario 2: Party B pushes Party A's torso from the front. Party A's right hand holds Party B's wrist and pulls it to the right. Meanwhile, Party A's body turns left, approaching Party B. The left hand holds Party B's neck, and the left leg forms an empty step, closely attaching to Party B's lower leg. Party A then rotates downward to the left and applies force, causing Party B to fall to the ground. (Figure 3-55 to 3-58)

场景2:乙方从正面推甲方躯干,甲方右手按住乙方手腕并向右侧带出,同时身体左转靠近乙方,左手按住乙方颈部,左腿虚步贴靠乙方的小腿部,同时向左下方旋转发力使乙方落空倒地(图3-55—3-58)。

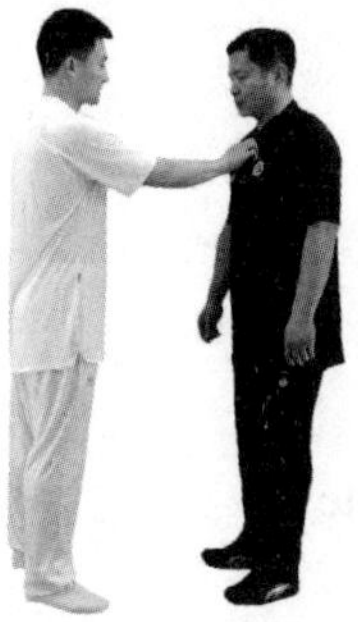
图 3–50

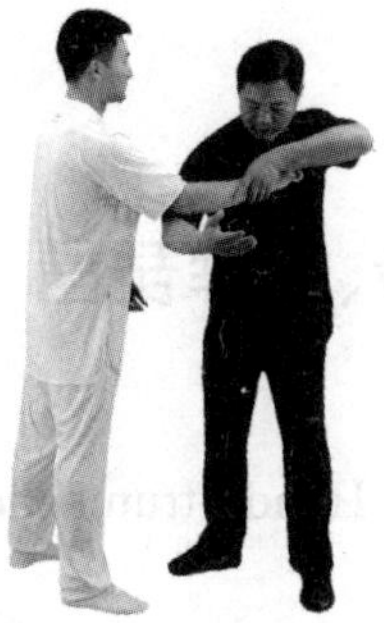
图 3–51

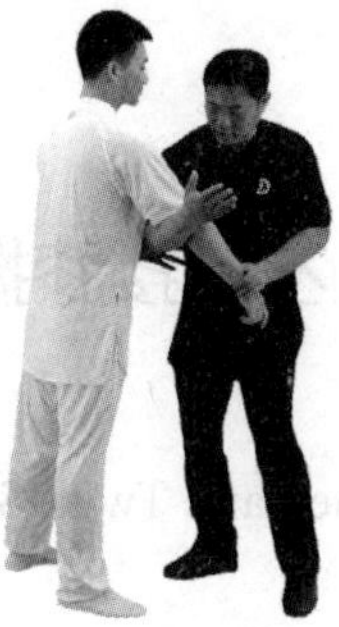
图 3–52

图 3–53

图 3–54

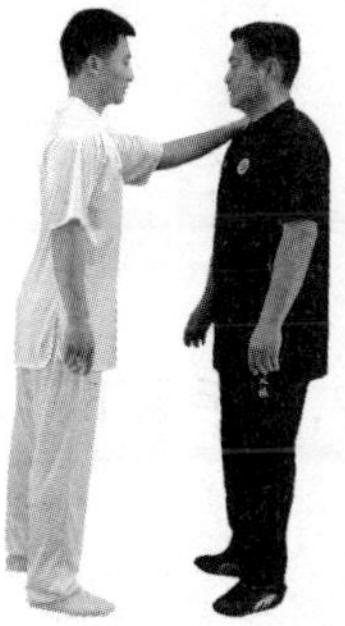
图 3–55

图 3–56

图 3–57

图 3–58

5. Insights on Styles

Unity and coordination of the whole body are essential to clearly demonstrate the transition from emptiness to solidity. Just like in the movements, teamwork also requires unity, clear division of tasks, coordination, and cooperation towards a common goal. By achieving unity and coordination, with determination to succeed and preparation to overcome all difficulties, individuals and teams can unleash their maximum potential. With faith in the people, strength in the country, and hope for the nation, we can work together as a unified force.

（五）招式感悟

周身一致，虚笼一转见分明，好的凌空来源于周身各部位的协调配合。动作如此，团队合作也是如此，做到团结协作，分工明确，各司其职，协调配合，向着一个目标共同努力，便能激发出团队的最大效能。我们每个人、每个团队都能做到有必胜的决心和战胜一切困难的准备，都把自己的能量发挥到最大，就能团结一致，众志成城，做到人民有信仰、国家有力量、民族有希望。

3–1

第二节 左右搂膝拗步、手挥琵琶

Section 2: Brush Knee and Twist Step，Hand Strums the Lute

Ⅰ. Brush Knee and Twist Step

1.Movement Explanation

（1）Follow the previous posture，turn to the left，lower the palm of the right hand，and raise the left hand（Figure 3-59 to 3-62）.

（2）Turn to the right，retract the left foot and touch the ground，supporting with the right palm（Figure 3-63 to 3-65）.

（3）Step forward with the left foot to the left side，lower the left palm，and bend the right arm（Figure 3-66）.

（4）Kick the leg and turn the waist to the left bow stance，embrace the left palm，and push with the right palm（Figure 3-67 and 3-68）.

Figure 3-59 to 3-62：Turn to the left and lower the palm

Figure 3-63 to 3-65：Lift the foot and support with the palm

Figure 3-66：Step forward and bend the arm

Figure 3-67 and 3-68：Kick and turn to the left in a bow stance

一、左右搂膝拗步

（一）动作图解

（1）接上式，左转，右手掌下落，左手上提（图3-59—3-62）。

（2）右转收左脚点地，托右掌（图3-63—3-65）。

（3）左脚左侧上步，左掌下落，右臂屈肘（图3-66）。

（4）蹬腿转腰成左弓步，左手搂掌，右手推掌（图3-67、3-68）。

图3-59—3-62 左转落掌
图3-63—3-65 收脚托掌
图3-66 出步屈臂
图3-67、3-68 弓步搂推

(5) Shift the weight backward, sit back and lift the foot, relax the arms and palms (Figure 3-69).

(5)重心后移,后坐撇脚,手臂手掌疏松(图 3-69)。

(6) Shift the weight forward, follow step and lift the right foot to touch the ground, support with the left palm (Figure 3-70 and 3-71).

(6)重心前移,跟步收右脚点地,托左掌(图 3-70、3-71)。

(7) Step to the right side with the right foot, lower the right palm, and bend the left arm (Figure 3-72).

(7)右脚右侧出步,右掌下落,左臂屈肘(图 3-72)。

(8) Kick the leg and turn the waist to the right bow stance, embrace the right palm, and push with the left palm (Figure 3-73 and 3-74).

(8)蹬腿转腰成右弓步,右手搂掌,左手推掌(图 3-73、3-74)。

Figure 3-69: Sit back and totate the foot outward

Figure 3-70、3-71: Shift weight forward and support with the palm

Figure 3-72: Step forward and bend the arm

Figure 3-73,3-74: Kick and turn to the right in a bow stance

图 3-69 后坐撇脚

图 3-70、3-71 收脚托掌

图 3-72 出步屈臂

图 3-73、3-74 弓步搂推

(9) Shift the weight backward, sit back and rotate the foot outward, relax the arms and palms (Figure 3-75).

(9)重心后移,后坐撇脚,手臂手掌疏松(图 3-75)。

(10) Shift the weight forward, follow step and lift the left foot to touch the ground, support with the right palm (Figure 3-76 and 3-77).

(10)重心前移,跟步收左脚点地,托右掌(图 3-76、3-77)。

(11) Step to the left side with the left foot, lower the left palm, and bend the right arm (Figure 3-78).

(11)左脚左侧出步,左掌下落,右臂屈肘(图 3-78)。

(12) Kick the leg and turn the waist to the left bow stance, embrace the left palm, and push with the right palm (Figure 3-79 and 3-80).

(12)蹬腿转腰成左弓步,左手搂掌,右手推掌(图 3-79、3-80)。

Figure 3-75：Sit back and rotate the foot outward

Figure 3-76 and 3-77：and support with the palm

Figure 3-78：Step forward and bend the arm

Figure 3-79 and 3-80：Kick and turn to the left in a bow stance

图 3-75 后坐撇脚

图 3-76、3-77 收脚托掌

图 3-78 出步屈臂

图 3-79、3-80 弓步搂推

图 3–59

图 3–60

图 3–61

图 3–62

图 3–63

图 3–64

图 3–65

图 3–66

图 3–67

图 3–68

图 3–69

图 3–70

图 3-71

图 3-72

图 3-73

图 3-74

图 3-75

图 3-76

图 3-77

图 3-78

图 3-79

图 3-80

2. Breathing Method

In the practice of “Brush Knee and Twist Step”, the breathing sequence is as follows: inhale when sitting back and lifting the foot, exhale when collecting the foot and supporting with the palm, inhale when stepping forward and bending the arm, exhale when pushing with the palm in a bow stance, and repeat this sequence.

（二）呼吸方法

“搂膝拗步”的演练呼吸顺序为：后坐撇脚吸气，收脚托掌呼气，上步屈臂吸气，弓步推掌呼气，以此循环。

3. Analysis of Power Pathway

When kicking the leg into a bow stance, the force is generated from the leg and

（三）劲路解析

蹬腿成弓步时，后腿蹬地发力促进转腰，前腿踩实支撑。以身促手，前手搂掌偏

distributed to the waist and spine, and then to the arms. Therefore, during the embracing and pushing movements, one should focus on experiencing the rotational effect of the torso. Brush Knee and Twist Step has a diagonal force, which involves rotational movements, emphasizing the central axis of the torso.

按，后手推掌掷放。

4.Examples of Practical Application

（四）实战应用举例

Party B pushes the torso of Party A with the right arm from the front. Party A holds Party B's wrist with the left hand and brings it to the right side, while simultaneously using the right hand to strike Party B's chest, neck, or face with a palm strike, causing Party B to be pushed away.（Figure 3-81 to 3-84）

乙方用右臂从正面推甲方躯干；甲方用左手将乙方手臂向右侧搂开，同时右手以掌推击对方胸口或颈部或面部，将对方击出（图 3-81—图 3-84）。

图 3-81

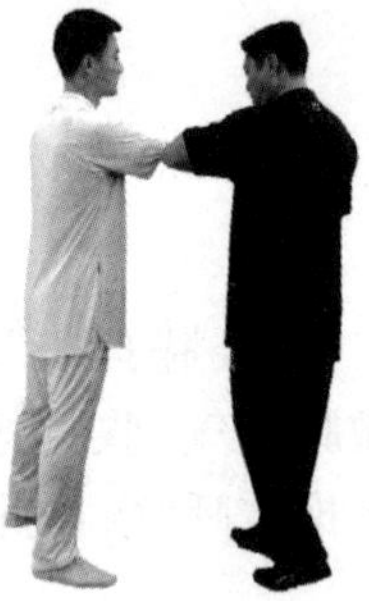
图 3-82

图 3-83

图 3-84

5. Insights on Styles

（五）招式感悟

The coordination of hand movements in "Brush Knee and Twist Step" allows for both softening and attacking. The pursuit of roundness and agility is essential. In

"搂膝拗步"，亦可柔化亦可进攻，圆活是追求，左顾右盼乃全面。"圆"文化也是一种为人处世之道，与人相处要温和谦逊，宽容忍让，敦厚处世，处理问题要圆通对待，柔中带刚，不卑不亢，不急不躁，进退有度。做

interpersonal relationships, one should be gentle, humble, tolerant, and sincere. When dealing with problems, a flexible and open-minded approach should be taken. It is important to be both soft and firm, calm and patient, and to have a sense of proportion in actions and decisions. This principle applies to both personal conduct and professional endeavors. Understanding the concept of "embracing all rivers" and grasping the balance between subjective initiative and objective laws will lead to greater effectiveness in both life and work.

人做事亦是如此,要懂得"海纳百川,有容乃大"的道理,把握分寸,掌握时机,把发挥主观能动性与客观规律有机结合起来,生活和工作都达到事半功倍的效果。

Ⅱ. Hand Strums the Lute

二、手挥琵琶

1.Movement Explanation

(一)动作图解

(1) Follow the previous posture, shift the weight forward, step with the back foot, and relax both hands (Figure 3-85).

(2) Sit back and lift the palm, lightly lift the front foot (Figure 3-86 and 3-87).

(3) Extend the front foot forward, with the back heel touching the ground, forming an empty stance. Both hands come together, supporting the palms, with the right hand joining at the left elbow joint (Figure 3-88).

(1)接上式,重心前移,后脚跟步,两手放松(图 3-85)。

(2)后坐挑掌,前脚轻轻拎起(图 3-86、3-87)。

(3)前脚前伸,脚后跟着地成虚步,两手合臂撑掌,右手合于左臂肘关节处(图 3-88)。

Figure 3-85: Step foot with relax hands

Figure 3-86 and 3-87: Sit back and lift the palm

Figure 3-88: Empty stance with arms joined

图 3-85 跟步松手

图 3-86、3-87 后坐挑掌

图 3-88 虚步合臂

图 3–85

图 3–86

图 3–87

图 3–88

2. Breathing Method

In continuation from "Brush Knee and Twist Step", inhale when sitting back and lifting the foot, exhale when forming the empty stance with joined arms.

3. Analysis of Power Pathway

When lifting the palm, the arms have a sense of drawing inward. When extending forward, there is a sense of outward projection. At the same time, the hands have the intention of inwardly capturing and seizing, while the front foot has a kicking and striking intention.

4. Examples of Practical Application

Party B uses the right arm to push Party A's torso from the front. Party A grabs Party B's wrist with the right hand, simultaneously rotates the body to the right, supports Party B's elbow joint with the left hand, exerts upward force, and lifts. Party A hooks the tip of the right foot tightly, lowers the heel,

（二）呼吸方法

接"搂膝拗步",跟步后坐吸气,虚步合臂呼气。

（三）劲路解析

挑掌时两臂有回引之意,前撑时有外放之意,同时两手有内合擒住之意,前脚有踢击之意。

（四）实战应用举例

乙方用右臂从正面推甲方躯干；甲方右手抓住乙方手腕,同时身体右转,左手托按对方肘关节、向上用力提挑,右脚脚尖勾紧、脚跟向下,踹击对方小腿,随后向下踩踏对方脚部,同时双手发力前推,使对方落空倒地(图 3-89—3-93)。

and kicks Party B's lower leg. Then, Party A steps down onto Party B's foot, while applying force with both hands to push forward, causing Party B to fall backward (Figure 3-89 to 3-93).

图 3–89

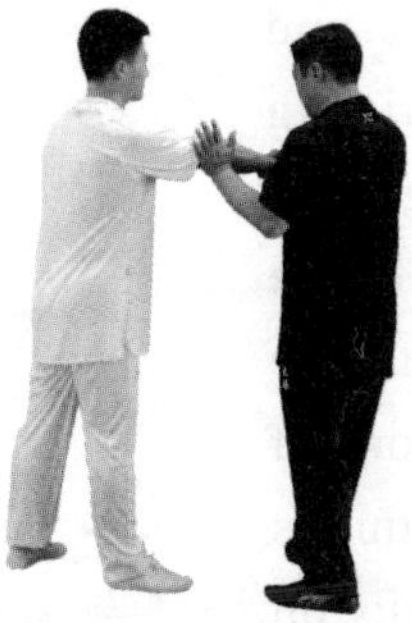

图 3–90

图 3–91

图 3–92

图 3–93

5. Insights on Styles

To control others without being controlled, capturing and seizing techniques are effective methods. The goal is to control the opponent without causing harm, and the key lies in the balance of force exerted by both hands. Communication should be stopped at an appropriate point, and etiquette is of utmost importance. In self-defense situations, actions should

（五）招式感悟

制人而不受制于人，擒拿是一种很好的方法。拿人而不伤人，力度全在两手称量。交流点到为止，礼为先。遇险自卫，则视情况而定。客观事物是多方面相互联系、发展变化的有机整体。做人做事要有系统思维，才能抓住整体，不失原则地采取灵活有效的方法处置事务。系统思维就是人们运用系统观点，把对象的互相联系的各个方面及其结构和功能进行系统认识的一种思维方法。

be based on the specific circumstances. Objective phenomena are interconnected, multifaceted, and constantly changing organic entities. In both personal conduct and professional endeavors, it is important to think systematically in order to grasp the whole picture and adopt flexible and effective approaches while maintaining principles. Systematic thinking is a cognitive method in which individuals use a systemic perspective to understand the various aspects, structures, and functions of objects in their interrelationships. It requires individuals to consider the whole, focus on the overall benefits and outcomes, and apply flexible methods as long as they align with the interests of the whole. This principle applies to life as well. By embracing the idea of "treating others kindly, sacrificing oneself for others, and embracing compassion", one can consider the overall situation and prioritize the greater good.

要求人们无论干什么事都要立足整体，把着眼点放在全局上，注重整体效益和整体结果。只要合于整体、全局的利益，就可以充分利用灵活的方法来处置。生活亦是如此，树立"善与人同，舍己从人，慈悲为念"的思想，顾全大局。

3-2

第三节　左右倒卷肱

Section 3: Reverse Wrapping of the Arm

1. Movement Explanation

(1) Follow the previous posture, the right hand unfolds backward from below, both hands flip and form an open palm in an empty stance. The center of the palms face

（一）动作图解

（1）接上式，右手由下往后展开，两手翻掌成虚步托掌，两掌心向上，前手胸前，后手斜向，后手略高于前手，两臂自然展开（图3-94、3-95）。

upward, with the front hand in front of the chest and the rear hand at a diagonal position slightly higher than the front hand. Both arms naturally extend (Figure 3-94 and 3-95).

(2) Lift the left foot and step forward with a knee strike, while the right arm bends at the elbow and closes the palm (Figure 3-96 and 3-97).

(2)左脚提膝后插步,右臂屈肘收掌(图3-96、3-97)。

(3) Rotate and sit back, the left hand circles back, and the right palm pushes forward (Figure 3-98).

(3)旋转后坐,左手回带,右掌前推(图3-98)。

(4) The left hand unfolds backward from below, both hands flip and form an open palm in an empty stance (the tip of the front foot touches the ground), with the front hand in front of the chest and the rear hand at a diagonal position slightly higher than the front hand. Both arms naturally extend (Figure 3-99).

(4)左手由下往后展开,两手翻掌成虚步(前脚脚尖点地)亮掌,前手胸前,后手斜向,后手略高于前手,两臂自然展开(图3-99)。

(5) Lift the right foot and step forward with a knee strike, while the left arm bends at the elbow and closes the palm (Figure 3-100 and 3-101).

(5)右脚提膝后插步,左臂屈肘收掌(图3-100、3-101)。

(6) Rotate and sit back, the right hand circles back, and the left palm pushes forward (Figure 3-102 and 3-103).

(6)旋转后坐,右手回带,左掌前推(图3-102、3-103)。

(7) The right hand unfolds backward from below, both hands flip and form an open palm in an empty stance (the tip of the front foot touches the ground) (Figure 3-104).

(7)右手由下往后展开,两手翻掌成虚步(前脚脚尖点地)托掌(图3-104)。

(8) Repeat the above movements on the left and right sides (Figure 3-105 to 3-111).

(8)上述动作,左右各再重复一次(图3-105—3-111)。

Figure 3-94 and 3-95：Empty Stance with Open Palms

Figure 3-96 and 3-97：Insert Step with Closed Palms

Figure 3-98：Sitting Back and Pushing Palms

Figure 3-99：Empty Stance with Open Palms

Figure 3-100 and 3-101：Insert Step with Closed Palms

Figure 3-102 and 3-103：Sitting Back and Pushing Palms

Figure 3-104：Empty Stance with Open Palms

Figure 3-105：Insert Step with Closed Palms

Figure 3-106：Sitting Back and Pushing Palms

Figure 3-107：Empty Stance with Open Palms

Figure 3-108 and 3-109：Insert Step with Closed Palms

Figure 3-110：Sitting Back and Pushing Palms

Figure 3-111：Empty Stance with Open Palms

图 3-94、3-95 虚步托掌
图 3-96、3-97 插步收掌
图 3-98 后坐推掌
图 3-99 虚步托掌
图 3-100、3-101 插步收掌
图 3-102、3-103 后坐推掌
图 3-104 虚步托掌
图 3-105 插步收掌
图 3-106 后坐推掌
图 3-107 虚步托掌
图 3-108、3-109 插步收掌
图 3-110 后坐推掌
图 3-111 虚步托掌

图 3–94

图 3–95

图 3–96

图 3–97

图 3–98

图 3-99

图 3-100

图 3-101

图 3-102

图 3-103

图 3-104

图 3-105

图 3-106

图 3-107

图 3-108

图 3-109

图 3-110

图 3-111

2. Breathing Method

In the sequence of movements, inhale as the right hand unfolds backward from below, exhale in the open palm with empty stance, inhale during the step forward with a knee strike and closing the palm, exhale in the sitting back and palm pushing movement. Inhale as the left hand unfolds backward from below, exhale in the open palm with empty stance, and continue the cycle.

3. Analysis of Power Pathway

During the process of transition from closing the palm to the palm pushing movement, rotate the foot and twist the leg, supporting the waist to drive the rotation of the torso. Then, the body's movement drives the arm's action. It is important not to forcefully pull or drag with the hands. Pay attention to experiencing the clever rotational effect of the body during the movement.

4. Examples of Practical Application

Party B uses the right arm to push Party A's torso from the front. Party A presses and pulls Party B's wrist with the right hand, pushes and presses Party B's shoulder with the left hand, and steps back with the right leg. At the same time, Party A turns Party B to the right and backward, causing Party B to lose balance and fall diagonally (Figure 3-112 to 3-115).

(二)呼吸方法

接手挥琵琶,右手向后展开吸气,虚步托掌呼气,后插步收掌吸气,后坐推掌呼气,左手向后展开吸气,虚步托掌呼气,以此循环。

(三)劲路解析

插步收掌到后坐推掌过程中,转脚拧腿,支撑腰部带动躯干的旋转,再由身躯带动手臂动作,千万不可手上硬拉硬拽。动作过程中注重体会身躯的巧妙旋转作用。

(四)实战应用举例

乙方用右臂从正面推甲方躯干;甲方右手按拉对方手腕,左手推按对方肩部,右腿向后撤步,同时将乙方向右后侧回带,使乙方失衡斜向倒地(图 3-112—3-115)。

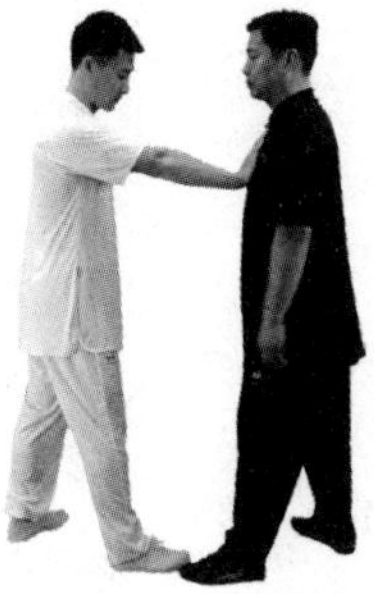

图 3-112

图 3-113

图 3-114

图 3-115

5. Insights on Styles

Attack can be executed during advancement, but it can also be executed during retreat. Whether to advance or retreat is not determined by oneself, but by the opponent. Retreat does not necessarily mean losing; taking a step back may lead to broader opportunities. In the process of understanding and transforming the world, it is crucial to firmly grasp the bottom line thinking. Based on our needs and objective conditions, we should clearly define and adhere to the bottom line, strive to resolve risks, avoid the worst outcomes, and strive to achieve the maximum expected value. In work, it is necessary to be prepared for the worst while striving for the best results. This approach allows us to be prepared and confident, firmly grasping the initiative. The same principle applies to life. One must understand the balance between firmness and flexibility. Life and learning are not about blindly forging ahead, but about knowing when to advance by retreating appropriately and maintaining a proper balance between tension and relaxation.

（五）招式感悟

进可攻，退亦可守，是进是退不在己，在人。退不一定是输，退一步也可能海阔天空。我们在认识世界和改造世界的过程中，要牢牢把握底线思维。根据我们的需要和客观的条件，划清并坚守底线，尽力化解风险，避免最坏结果，同时争取实现最大期望值。工作中凡事从坏处准备，努力争取最好的结果。这样才能有备无患、遇事不慌，牢牢把握主动权。生活亦是如此，要懂得刚柔相济，生活和学习并不是一味地勇往直前，而是需要在适当的时候以退为进，把握好张弛有度。

3-3

第四节 左右揽雀尾

Section 4: Embracing the Sparrow's Tail on the Left and Right

Ⅰ. Embracing the Sparrow's Tail on the Left

1. Movement Explanation

(1) Following the previous movement of sitting back and pushing palms, the left foot touches the ground, the left hand arcs downward, and the right hand arcs upward to form a ball in front of the chest (Figure 3-116).

(2) Slightly turn the body to the left and step forward with the left foot (Figure 3-117).

(3) Extend the left hand forward and upward while assuming the left bow stance, with the forearm horizontally positioned in front of the body, and the right hand pressing down to the side of the waist (Figure 3-118).

(4) Pull the right hand forward, then both hands flip over and retract towards the right side while sitting back (Figure 3-119 and 3-120).

(5) Turn the body to the left and align it properly, with the right arm folded inside the left arm (Figure 3-121 and 3-122).

(6) Assume a bow stance and push forward with both arms (Figure 3-123).

一、左揽雀尾

(一)动作图解

(1)接上式的虚步托掌,左脚顺势收脚点地,左手向下画弧,右手向上画弧成胸前抱球(图3-116)。

(2)身体微左转,出左脚上步(图3-117)。

(3)蹬腿成左弓步,左手前上掤出,前臂横对身体,右手下按至腰胯旁(图3-118)。

(4)右手前引,随后两手翻掌向右后方回捋,后坐步(图3-119、3-120)。

(5)身体左转坐正,右手屈臂折叠于左手内侧(图3-121、3-122)。

(6)蹬腿成弓步,两臂合力前挤(图3-123)。

(7) Expand both palms, sit back with flexed hips, and press down (Figure 3-124 to 3-126).

(8) Lift both palms in front of the chest, and push forward with a bow stance (Figure 3-127).

(7) 两掌展开,后坐屈胯下按(图3-124—3-126)。

(8) 两掌上提于胸前,弓步前推(图3-127)。

Figure 3-116: Collecting the Foot and Holding the Ball

Figure 3-117: Turning to the Left and Stepping Out

Figure 3-118: Bow Stance with Forward Extension

Figure 3-119: Extending the Hand Forward

Figure 3-120: Retracting While Sitting Back

Figure 3-121 and 3-122: Turning to the Left and Joining Hands

Figure 3-123: Forward Squeeze in a Bow Stance

Figure 3-124 and 3-125: Expanding Both Palms

Figure 3-126: Bending the Hips and Retracting

Figure 3-127: Forward Press in a Bow Stance

图 3-116 收脚抱球

图 3-117 左转出步

图 3-118 弓步前掤

图 3-119 伸手前引

图 3-120 后坐回捋

图 3-121、3-122 左转合手

图 3-123 弓步前挤

图 3-124、3-125 两掌展开

图 3-126 屈胯回引

图 3-127 弓步前按

图 3-116

图 3-117

图 3-118

图 3-119

图 3-120

图 3-121

图 3-122

图 3-123

图 3-124

图 3-125

图 3-126

图 3-127

2. Breathing Method

Inhale while collecting the foot and making the arc, exhale while holding the ball. Inhale while stepping forward with the left foot and extending the arm forward, exhale while pressing down during the retraction. Inhale while turning the body and joining the hands, exhale while squeezing forward in a bow stance. Inhale while expanding and retracting, exhale while pressing forward in a bow stance.

（二）呼吸方法

收脚画弧吸气，抱球呼气，左脚上步吸气，前掤呼气，前引吸气，右下回捋呼气，转身合手吸气，弓步前挤呼气，展开回引吸气，弓步前按呼气。

3. Analysis of Power Pathway

The power originates from the feet and is conveyed through the waist and hips. Embracing the Sparrow's Tail focuses on the four main powers: ward-off, rollback, press, and push. When executing the movements, attention should be given to the role of the legs, waist, and hips. Flexibility and adaptation are required, avoiding excessive leaning forward or backward to prevent being exploited. Furthermore, it is essential to maintain the awareness of ward-off in the forearm, rollback in the palm, press on the back of the hand, and push in the heel of the hand.

（二）劲路解析

劲起于脚，运转于腰胯。揽雀尾主要是掤、捋、挤、按四正劲，行拳运劲时要注重腿、腰、胯的作用，需转则转，需屈则屈，往前上体不可过分前俯，往后不可后仰，以免被借势借力。另要有掤在前臂，捋在掌心，挤在手背，按在掌跟的意识。

4. Examples of Practical Application

In an encounter, Party B uses the right arm to push Party A's torso from the front.

（四）实战应用举例

乙方用右臂从正面推甲方躯干；甲方左手按住乙方右手手腕，右脚上步，右手贴

Party A uses the left hand to hold Party B's right wrist, steps forward with the right foot, and brings the right hand close to Party B's right armpit. By exerting force, Party B is thrown off to the side, causing Party B to lose balance and fall (Figure 3-128 to 3-130).

靠乙方右侧腋下,同时发力将对方向外侧撇开,使乙方落空倒地(图 3-128—3-130)。

If Party A fails to knock down Party B, Party A can utilize force from the top to strike backward. Party A changes hands, the left hand switches to a grasping position, while the right hand flips over to press Party B's upper arm. Party A then pulls downward and outward to make Party B lose balance and fall (Figure 3-131 and 3-132).

未将对方击倒。乙方发力前顶,则借力向后打;甲方换手,左手变按为托抓,右手翻掌按住乙方上臂,往左侧下方捋带,使乙方失衡倒地(图 3-131、3-132)。

If Party A fails to knock down Party B, Party A can hold onto Party B's exerted force. Party A quickly uses both hands to exert force forward, targeting Party B's chest and abdomen, causing Party B to lose balance and retreat (Figure 3-133 and 3-134).

未将对方击倒。乙方发力拉住,则甲方借力快速用两手相合向前挤打乙方胸腹部,使乙方失衡后退(图 3-133、3-134)。

If Party A fails to knock down Party B, Party A can push forward with both hands. Party B's upper arm is flipped and pressed by both hands from the outside, and then pulled back and pressed down, resulting in Party B falling empty (Figure 3-135 to 3-137).

未将对方击倒。乙方发力双手前推,则甲方双手从外侧翻掌按乙方上臂,回拉下按,使乙方落空倒地(图 3-135—3-137)。

If Party B resists Party A's force from behind, Party A uses Party B's resistance to push forward with both hands, causing Party B to fall empty (Figure 3-138 and 3-139).

未将对方击倒。乙方向后发力相持,则甲方借力用双手前推乙方,使乙方落空倒地(图 3-138、3-139)。

图 3–128

图 3–129

图 3–130

图 3–131

图 3–132

图 3–133

图 3–134

图 3–135

图 3–136

图 3–137

图 3–138

图 3–139

5. Insights on Styles

Ward-off, rollback, press, and push should be executed with meticulous attention while maintaining balance and proper posture. This principle applies not only to Tai Chi movements but also to our actions and endeavors in life. A comprehensive approach is essential. Establishing a global perspective and focusing on the overall situation while recognizing the importance of individual contributions are crucial for promoting overall development. Understanding and managing the relationship between the whole and its parts are of significant guiding significance in our practice. Firstly, when handling tasks, we should consider the overall situation and strive for optimal objectives. Secondly, pay attention to the details and ensure that individual components fulfill their roles, facilitating the maximization of overall functionality.

（五）招式感悟

掤、捋、挤、按需认真，平正方圆为核心。行拳走架是如此，做人做事亦是如此，面面俱到方为上策。要树立全局观念，立足整体，同时重视部分作用，搞好局部，促进整体发展。要理解并处理好整体和部分的相互关系，这对于我们的实践具有重要的指导意义：首先，办事情要从整体着眼，寻求最优目标；其次，搞好局部，使整体功能得到最大限度的发挥。

Ⅱ. Embracing the Sparrow's Tail on the Right

二、右揽雀尾

1. Movement Explanation

（一）动作图解

(1) Continuing from the previous movement, turn to the right, hook the left foot, and extend the right hand in front (Figure 3-140).

(2) Step forward with the right foot, touching the ground, while the right hand arcs downward and the left hand folds in front of the chest, forming a ball (Figure 3-141 and 3-142).

(3) Slightly turn the body to the right

（1）接上式，右转身，扣左脚，右手面前拉开（图 3-140）。

（2）右脚蹬地收脚点地，右手向下画弧，左手收于胸前成胸前抱球（图 3-141、3-142）。

（3）身体微右转，出右脚上步（图

and step forward with the right foot (Figure 3-143).

3-143)。

(4) Flex the leg to assume a right bow stance, extend the right hand forward and upward, with the forearm horizontally positioned in front of the body, and the left hand pressing down to the side of the waist (Figure 3-144 and 3-145).

(4)蹬腿成右弓步,右手前上掤出,前臂横对身体,左手下按至腰胯旁(图 3-144、3-145)。

(5) Pull the left hand forward, then both hands flip over and retract towards the left side while sitting back and stepping back (Figure 3-146 to 3-148).

(5)左手前引,随后两手翻掌向左后方回捋,后坐步(图 3-146—3-148)。

(6) Turn the body to the right and align it properly, with the left arm folded inside the right arm (Figure 3-149 and 3-150).

(6)身体右转坐正,左手屈臂折叠于右手内侧(图 3-149、3-150)。

(7) Assume a bow stance and push forward with both arms (Figure 3-151, 3-152).

(7)蹬腿成弓步,两臂合力前挤(图 3-151、3-152)。

(8) Expand both palms, sit back with flexed hips, and press down (Figure 3-153 to 3-155).

(8)两掌展开,后坐屈胯下按(图 3-153—3-155)。

(9) Lift both palms in front of the chest and push forward with a bow stance (Figure 3-156).

(9)两掌上提于胸前,弓步前推(图 3-156)。

Figure 3-140: Turning to the Right with Splitting Palms

Figure 3-141 and 3-142: Foot Closure and Ball Embrace

Figure 3-143: Turning to the Right and Step Out

Figure 3-144 and 3-145: Bow Stance with Forward Ward-off

图 3-140 右转分掌

图 3-141、3-142 收脚抱球

图 3-143 右转出步

图 3-144、3-145 弓步前棚

Figure 3-146: Forward Extension of the Hand

Figure 3-147 and 3-148: Sitting Back and Pulling Back

Figure 3-149 and 3-150: Turning to the Right and Joining Hands

Figure 3-151 and 3-152: Bow Stance with Forward Squeezing

Figure 3-153 and 3-154: Expansion of Both Palms

Figure 3-155: Flexing the Hips and Pulling Back

Figure 3-156: Forward Press in a Bow Stance

图 3-146 伸手前引

图 3-147、3-148 后坐回捋

图 3-149、3-150 右转合手

图 3-151、3-152 弓步前挤

图 3-153、3-154 两掌展开

图 3-155 屈胯回引

图 3-156 弓步前按

图 3–140

图 3–141

图 3–142

图 3–143

图 3–144

图 3–145

图 3–146

图 3–147

图 3–148

图 3–149

图 3–150

图 3–151

图 3–152

图 3–153

图 3–154

图 3–155

图 3–156

2. Breathing Method

Inhale while turning the body and separating the palms, exhale while holding the ball. Inhale while stepping forward with the right foot and extending the arm forward, exhale while pushing forward. Inhale while pulling back with the left hand and sitting back, exhale while turning the body and joining the hands. Inhale while squeezing forward in a bow stance, exhale while expanding and retracting. Inhale while lifting and pulling back, exhale while pressing forward in a bow stance.

（二）呼吸方法

转身分掌吸气，抱球呼气，右脚上步吸气，前掤呼气，前引吸气，左下回捋呼气，转身合手吸气，弓步前挤呼气，展开回引吸气，弓步前按呼气。

3–4

3.Analysis of Power Pathway, Examples of Practical Application, and Insights on Styles

Please refer to the analysis of power pathway, combat application examples, and insights on techniques for Embracing the Sparrow's Tail on the Left.

（三）劲路解析、实战应用举例、招式感悟

劲路解析、实战应用、招式感悟参考左揽雀尾。

第五节　单鞭、云手、单鞭

Section 5: Single Whip, Cloud Hands, Single Whip

Ⅰ. Single Whip

一、单鞭

1.Movement Explanation

（一）动作图解

（1）Continuing from the previous movement, push off with the right leg and turn to the left. Lift the right toe and point it inward. Left hand flips the palm and moves to the left in front of the chest, palm facing outward. Right palm presses down towards the left palm, palm facing downward (Figure 3-157 to 3-159).

（2）Press down with the left hand and lift up with the right hand. Push off with the left leg towards the right with cloud hands. Right palm faces inward, left palm faces downward (Figure 3-160 to 3-162).

（3）Naturally bring down the left foot, flip the right palm and hook with the fingertips pointing downwards. The right arm is diagonally raised to shoulder height

（1）接上式，蹬右腿左转身，右脚尖抬起内扣，左手翻掌胸前向左云掌，掌心向外，右掌下按往左云掌，掌心向下（图 3-157—3-159）。

（2）左手下按右手上提，蹬左脚往右云掌，右掌心向内，左掌心向下（图 3-160—3-162）。

（3）顺势收左脚点地，右手翻掌抓勾，勾尖朝下，右臂肩高斜向，自然伸开；左掌松手上提，掌心向内（图 3-163、3-164）。

and naturally extended. Release tension from the left hand and lift it up with the palm facing inward (Figure 3-163 and 3-164).

(4) Turn the body to the left, step up to the left side with the left foot, and bring the left hand to the front of the chest (Figure 3-165).

(5) Flip the left palm while kicking with the leg, and perform a single palm push in a left bow stance (Figure 3-166).

Figure 3-157 to 3-159: Left Cloud Hands

Figure 3-160 to 3-162: Right Cloud Hands

Figure 3-163, 3-164: Hooking and Lifting the Palm

Figure 3-165: Stepping Up with the Palm

Figure 3-166: Pushing the Palm in a Bow Stance

（4）身体左转，左脚左侧上步，左手带至胸前(图 3-165)。

（5）蹬腿翻左掌，左弓步单推掌(图 3-166)。

图 3-157—3-159 左云掌

图 3-160—3-162 右云掌

图 3-163、3-164 抓勾提掌

图 3-165 上步带掌

图 3-166 弓步推掌

图 3–157

图 3–158

图 3–159

图 3–160

图 3–161

图 3-162　　图 3-163　　图 3-164　　图 3-165　　图 3-166

2. Breathing Method

Inhale during the left turn of the cloud hands, exhale when changing hands up and down. Inhale during the right turn of the cloud hands, exhale during the hooking and lifting of the palm. Inhale when stepping up with the palm, exhale during the palm push in a bow stance.

3. Analysis of Power Pathway

The waist should turn smoothly and dynamically. The hooking action should have a sense of pulling and drawing inward. The stepping should be light and agile, and the palm push should have a sense of throwing and releasing. The power originates from the feet, passes through the spine, and extends to the hands.

4. Examples of Practical Application

Scenario 1: Party B uses the left arm to push Party A's torso from the front. Party

(二)呼吸方法

左转云掌吸气,上下换手呼气,右转云掌吸气,抓勾提掌呼气,上步带掌吸气,弓步推掌呼气。

(三)劲路解析

转腰要圆活,抓勾回带有引化之意。迈步要轻灵,推掌有掷放之意,力由脚起,经由脊背,达于手。

(四)实战应用举例

场景 1: 乙方用左臂从正面推甲方躯

A grabs Party B's forearm with the right hand and applies force from the inside to the front, striking the opponent's neck with the palm (Figure 3-167 to 3-171).

Scenario 2: Party B uses the left arm to push Party A's torso from the front. Party A grabs Party B's forearm with the right hand and hooks Party B's neck from below. Party B exerts force to push Party A forward, causing Party A to lose balance and fall backward (Figure 3-172 to 3-176).

干；甲方右手抓住乙方前臂，左手从内侧由后向前发力，用手掌击打对方颈部（图3-167—3-171）。

场景2：乙方用左臂从正面推甲方躯干；甲方右手抓住乙方前臂，左手勾住对方脖子下收，乙方向后发力挣脱，甲方借力将乙方向前推出，使乙方落空倒地（图3-172—3-176）。

图3-167

图3-168

图3-169

图3-170

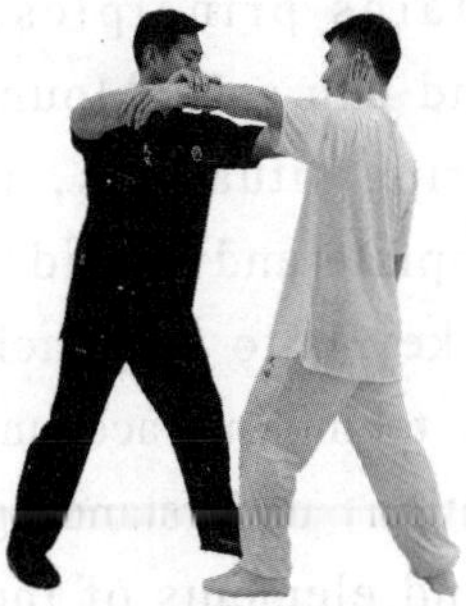
图3-171

图 3-172

图 3-173

图 3-174

图 3-175

图 3-176

5. Insights on Styles

(五)招式感悟

Each move contains principles, and even a single hand can split Mount Hua. When encountering situations, it is important to contemplate and consider various methods. The key is to approach things comprehensively, taking into account the entirety of the situation, understanding the interconnections and elements of the system, and conducting comprehensive analysis, optimization, and combination to achieve a complete and accurate understanding of the matter. We should continuously strengthen our awareness of problems, adhere to specific analysis of concrete issues, be adept at understanding and resolving contradictions, and prioritize

一招一式皆有道,单手也能劈华山。遇事多琢磨,万法巧为先。做人做事亦是如此,用综合的思维方式来认识事物,既要着眼于事物的整体,从整体出发认识事物和系统,又要把事物和系统的各个部分、各个要素联系起来进行考察,统筹考虑,优化组合,最终形成关于这一事物的完整准确的认识。我们要不断强化问题意识,坚持具体问题具体分析,善于认识和化解矛盾,尤其是优先解决主要矛盾作为打开局面的突破口,以此带动其他矛盾的解决。

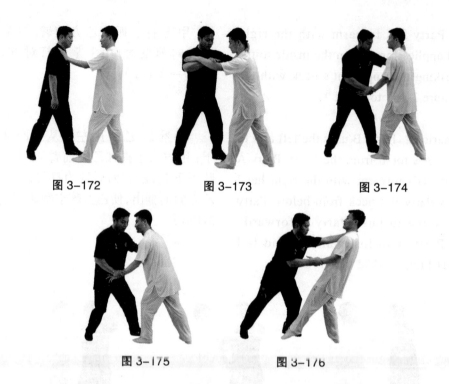

resolving the main contradictions as a breakthrough to facilitate the resolution of other contradictions.

Ⅱ. Cloud Hands

1.Movement Explanation

(1) Continuing from the previous movement, push off with the left foot and turn to the right. Point the left toe inward and move the left hand from below to the right in a cloud palm position (Figure 3-177).

(2) Lift the left palm with the palm facing inward. The right hand changes to a hooking palm and presses downward. Perform a left cloud palm motion and naturally bring the right foot together (Figure 3-178 to 3-180).

(3) Lift the right palm with the palm facing inward. Flip the left palm and press downward. Perform a right cloud palm motion and step out with the left foot (Figure 3-178 to 3-181).

(4) Lift the left palm with the palm facing inward. Flip the right palm and press downward. Perform a left cloud palm motion and naturally bring the right foot together (Figure 3-182 and 3-183).

(5) Lift the right palm with the palm facing inward. Flip the left palm and press downward. Perform a right cloud palm motion and step out with the left foot (Figure 3-184, 3 and 185).

(6) Lift the left palm with the palm facing inward. Flip the right palm and press downward. Perform a left cloud palm motion

二、云手

(一)动作图解

(1)接上式,蹬左脚右转,左脚尖内扣,左手由下往右云掌(图 3-177)。

(2)左掌上提,掌心向内,右手勾变掌下按,左云掌,顺势收右脚合步(图 3-178—3-180)。

(3)右掌上提,掌心向内,左掌翻掌下按,右云掌,左脚出步(图 3-178—3-181)。

(4)左掌上提,掌心向内,右掌翻掌下按,左云掌,顺势收右脚合步(图 3-182、3-183)。

(5)右掌上提,掌心向内,左掌翻掌下按,右云掌,左脚出步(图 3-184、3-185)。

(6)左掌上提,掌心向内,右掌翻掌下按,左云掌,顺势收右脚合步(图 3-186—3-188)。

and naturally bring the right foot together (Figure 3-186 to 3-188).

Figure 3-177: Right Cloud, Left Palm

Figure 3-178—3-180: Left Cloud Palm with Foot Together

Figure 3-178—3-181: Right Cloud Palm with Foot Stepping Out

Figure 3-182, 3-183: Left Cloud Palm with Foot Together

Figure 3-184, 3-185: Right Cloud Palm with Foot Stepping Out

Figure 3-186—3-188: Left Cloud Palm with Foot Together

图 3-177 右云左掌
图 3-178—3-180 左云掌合步
图 3-178—3-181 右云掌出步
图 3-182、3-183 左云掌合步
图 3-184、3-185 右云掌出步
图 3-186—3-188 左云掌合步

图 3–177

图 3–178

图 3–179

图 3–180

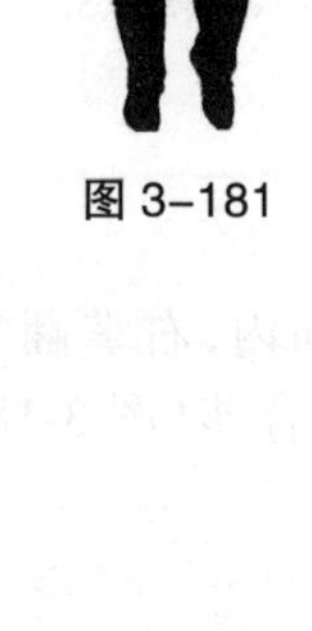

图 3–181

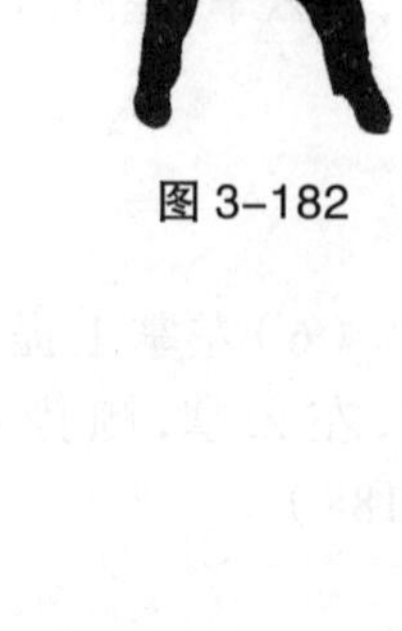

图 3–182

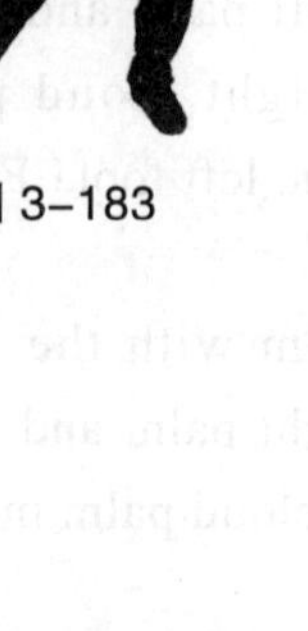

图 3–183

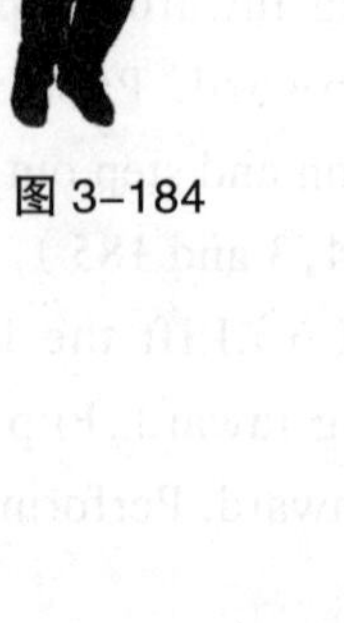

图 3–184

图 3–185

图 3–186

图 3–187

图 3–188

2. Breathing Method

Inhale while turning the body to the right with the left toe pointing inward. Exhale during the left cloud palm motion with the feet together. Inhale during the right cloud palm motion with the foot stepping out. Exhale during the left cloud palm motion with the feet together. Inhale during the right cloud palm motion with the foot stepping out. Exhale during the left cloud palm motion with the feet together.

3. Analysis of Power Pathway

The upper hand is at chest height, while the lower hand is at the lower abdomen. The leg movement and waist rotation should be coordinated with the hand movements. Clear differentiation between substantial and insubstantial, and lightness in stepping. The entire body moves as one unit. The movements should be smooth, rounded, and flexible.

（二）呼吸方法

左脚尖内扣右转身吸气，左云掌合步呼气，右云掌出步吸气，左云掌合步呼气，右云掌出步吸气，左云掌合步呼气。

（三）劲路解析

上手胸前高度，下手小腹高度。蹬腿转腰，以身带手。虚实转换明了，迈步轻灵。一动俱动，周身一致。摇转圆活，柔化万千。

4. Examples of Practical Application

Party B uses the left hand to strike Party A from the front. Party A performs cloud hands movements to block Party B's attack. After blocking, Party A switches the power between the hands, pressing down with the right hand and striking the elbow joint with an upward motion of the left hand, immobilizing Party B. Then, Party A exerts force to the left, throwing Party B off balance (Figure 3-189 to 3-192).

（四）实战应用举例

乙方用左手从正面击打甲方；甲方身体左右转动云手格挡对方攻击。格挡攻击后，甲方双手上下交换发力，右手下按手腕，左手上挑击打肘关节，使乙方被钳制，随后发力向左侧甩送（图 3-189—3-192）。

图 3-189

图 3-190

图 3-191

图 3-192

5. Insights on Styles

Cloud in the hands, movement in the body. Cloud hands may seem like a hand technique, but it involves the entire body. It is important to see through appearances and focus on essence, avoiding the confusion of priorities. This applies to life as well. One should conduct oneself with integrity and righteousness, and act with honesty and fairness. "Standing tall and unyielding, without desires, one is firm." In life

（五）招式感悟

云在手，运在身。看似云手，实则云身。透过表象看本质，切不可本末倒置。生活亦是如此，做人要堂堂正正，充满正气，做事要光明磊落，不趋炎附势。"壁立千仞，无欲则刚"，在生活和工作中要有正当的见解。

and work, one should have reasonable perspectives.

Ⅲ. Single Whip

1.Movement Explanation

(1) Continuing from the previous movement, proceed with the right cloud hands motion. Flip the right hand into a hooking palm and grab, while lifting the left hand with the palm facing upward. The left toe lightly touches the ground (Figure 3-193, Figure 3-194).

(2) Slightly turn the body to the left, lift the left foot and take a step forward, bringing the left palm to the front of the chest (Figure 3-195).

(3) Flip the left palm and push forward with the palm in a bow stance (Figure 3-196).

Figure 3-193: Right Cloud Palm
Figure 3-194: Hooking Palm with Lifting Hand
Figure 3-195: Step Forward with Palm
Figure 3-196: Pushing Palm in Bow Stance

三、单鞭

(一)动作图解

(1)接上式,继续右云手,右手翻掌抓勾,左手提掌,左脚尖虚点(图 3-193、图 3-194)。

(2)身体微左转,提左脚迈步,左掌带至胸前(图 3-195)。

(3)左手翻掌,弓步前推掌(图 3-196)。

图 3-193 右云掌
图 3-194 抓勾提掌
图 3-195 迈步带掌
图 3-196 弓步推掌

图 3–193

图 3–194

图 3–195

图 3–196

2. Breathing Method

(二)呼吸方法

Continuing from the previous movement, inhale during the right cloud palm motion, exhale during the hooking palm with lifting hand, inhale during the step forward with palm, and exhale during the pushing palm in bow stance.

接上式,右云掌吸气,抓勾提掌呼气,迈步带掌吸气,弓步推掌呼气。

3. Analysis of Power Pathway, and Examples of Practical Application

(三)劲路解析、实战应用举例

Please refer to the ninth movement, Single Whip.

参考第九式单鞭。

4. Insights on Styles

(四)招式感悟

"There's always a way as long as you maintain in good a state of mind." With the right approach, tasks can be accomplished with less effort. With the wrong approach, efforts may be doubled while results are halved, leading to futile outcomes. Passion alone is not enough to succeed in a task; it merely reflects the attitude towards doing it. Adopting the correct methods is the key to achieving success. Good work methods help individuals grasp the essence of things, solve problems quickly, and improve work efficiency. Albert Einstein once said, "Success = Hard work + Right methods + Less empty talk." Having effective methods is crucial.

"只要思想不滑坡,办法总比困难多。"方法得当,事半功倍。方法不当,事倍功半,徒劳无益。想要做成一件事情,仅有热情是不够的,有热情只是具备了想干事的态度,采用正确方法才是干成事的保证。好的工作方法可以帮助人们抓住事物的关键,快速解决问题,提高工作效率。爱因斯坦曾讲过:成功=艰苦地劳动+正确的方法+少谈空话。好方法很重要。

3–5

第六节　高探马、右蹬脚、双峰贯耳

Section 6: High Pat on Horse, Kicking with Right Heel, Strike to Ears with Both Fists

Ⅰ. High Pat on Horse

1.Movement Explanation

(1) Step the right foot forward into a heel-toe stance while both hands loosen and flip with the palms slanting upward (Figure 3-197 and 3-198).

(2) Shift the weight backward, slightly lift the front foot, and bend the right arm to bring it close to the shoulder (Figure 3-199).

(3) Extend the front foot forward, placing the toes on the outer side to form an empty stance. Push forward with the right palm, while the left palm gathers in front of the abdomen with the palm facing upward (the hand position is concealed by the body, not visible) (Figure 3-200).

Figure 3-197 and 3-198: Heel-toe Stance with Flipping Palms

Figure 3-199: Lifting Foot with Gathering Palm

Figure 3-200: Empty Stance with Pushing Palm

一、高探马

（一）动作图解

（1）右脚前移跟步，两手松手翻掌，掌心斜向上（图 3-197、3-198）。

（2）重心后坐，前脚微提，右掌屈臂收于肩上（图 3-199）。

（3）前脚前伸脚尖外侧着地成虚步，右掌前推，左掌收于腹前，掌心向上（身体遮挡住，看不到手型）（图 3-200）。

图 3-197、3-198 跟步翻掌

图 3-199 提脚收掌

图 3-200 虚步推掌

图 3-197

图 3-198

图 3-199

图 3-200

2. Breathing Method

Continuing from the previous movement, inhale during the heel-toe stance with loosening hands, exhale as the foot lands and the palms flip, inhale while lifting the foot and gathering the palms, exhale during the empty stance with pushing palm.

（二）呼吸方法

接上式，跟步松手吸气，落脚翻掌呼气，提脚收掌吸气，虚步推掌呼气。

3. Analysis of Power Pathway

The left hand signifies drawing back and leading, while the right hand signifies pushing forward and surging ahead. Both hands support each other in the front and back movements. Additionally, the hands can also rotate left and right, symbolizing the toppling of the "horse's head."

（三）劲路解析

左手有回带回引之意，右手有前推前挫之意，两手前后对撑。除此之外，两手也可有左右翻转，扳倒"马头"之意。

4. Examples of Practical Application

Party B uses the left arm to push the torso of Party A from the front. Party A's left hand wraps around Party B's right arm from the inside to the outside, trapping Party B's arm under the armpit. At the same time,

（四）实战应用举例

乙方用左臂从正面推甲方躯干；甲方左手由内向外绕缠乙方右臂，将乙方手臂夹在腋下，同时左手拖住对方肘关节，右手右

Party A's left hand grabs Party B's elbow joint, and the right hand strikes forward with the palm, targeting Party B's chin, face, abdomen, or grabbing the neck area (Figure 3-201 to 3-206).

后向前,用手掌击打乙方下颌或面部或腹部或者卡住颈部。(图 3-201—3-206)

图 3-201

图 3-202

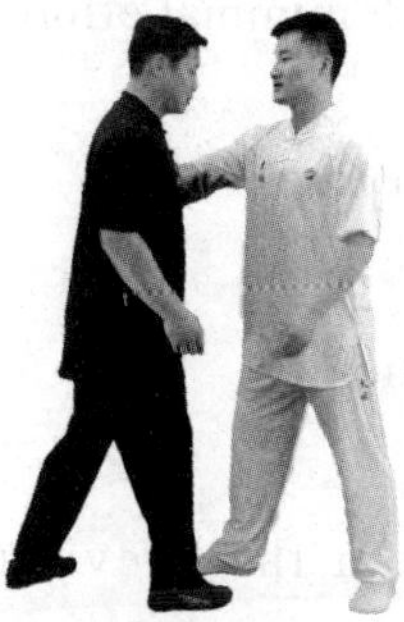
图 3-203

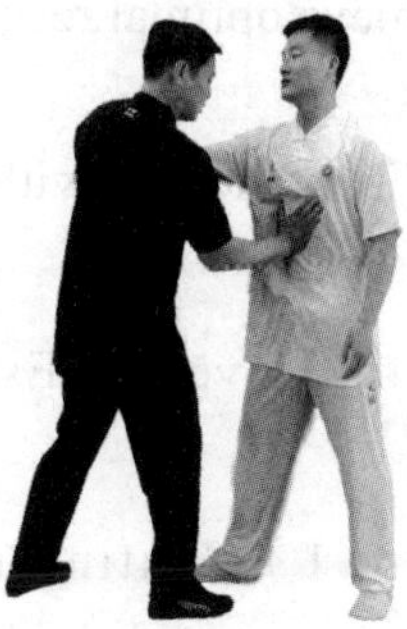
图 3-204

图 3-205

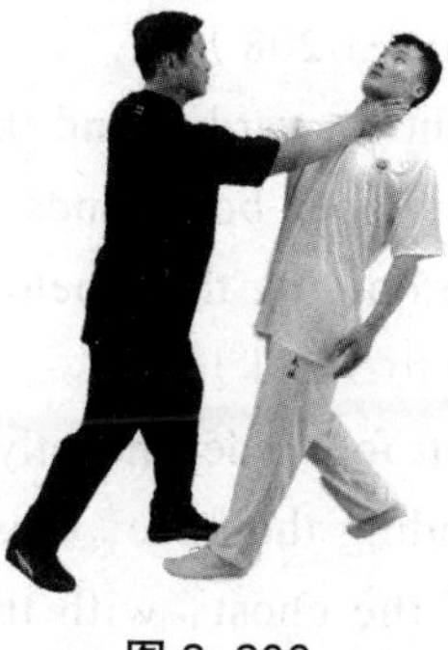
图 3-206

5. Insights on Styles

(五)招式感悟

"Capture the leader first to control the whole group; control the head to dominate the entire body." When thinking and working, we should firmly grasp the main aspect of the contradiction, distinguishing between primary and secondary, and not lose sight of the big picture due to minor

"擒贼先擒王,制人先制首。头领周身,降首则制全身。"想问题、办事情,应该牢牢抓住矛盾的主要方面,不能主次不分,因小失大。在实际工作中,我们要坚持矛盾的客观性,就是要弄清当时当地客观存在的矛盾是什么,从而采取正确的解决方法,以收到事半功倍的效果。

details. In practical work, we should adhere to the objectivity of contradictions, that is, understanding the specific contradictions present at the time and place, in order to adopt the correct approach for resolution and achieve optimal results with minimal effort.

Ⅱ. Kicking with Right Heel

二、右蹬脚

1.Movement Explanation

(一)动作图解

(1) Continuing from the previous movement, lift the left foot and step forward to the left front. The left hand passes through above the right hand with the palm facing upward (Figure 3-207 and 3-208).

(1)接上式,提左脚向左前方迈步,左手从右手上方穿掌(图 3-207、3-208)。

(2) Shift the weight forward, bend the left leg, squat down, and open both hands in a circular motion while holding them below the waist (Figure 3-209 to 3-211).

(2)重心前移,左腿屈膝下蹲,两手打开画圆下捧(图 3-209—3-211)。

(3) Stand on the left foot independently, lift the right leg by bending the knee, cross both hands in front of the chest, with the right hand on the outside (Figure 3-212).

(3)左脚独立,右腿屈膝上提,两手胸前交叉合抱,右手在外(图 3-212)。

(4) Flip both hands and open them, palms facing forward, while the right heel kicks out to the right front and the toes are retracted (Figure 3-213).

(4)两手翻掌平抹打开,立掌掌心向前,右脚向右前方蹬出,收脚尖(图 3-213)。

Figure 3-207 and 3-208: Foot Landing and Penetrating Palms

Figure 3-209 to 3-211: Squatting Down and Supporting

Figure 3-212: Lifting Knee and Embracing Palms

Figure 3-213: Kicking the Right Heel and Separating Palms

图 3-207、3-208 落脚穿掌

图 3-209—3-211 屈膝下捧

图 3-212 提膝抱掌

图 3-213 蹬右脚分掌

图 3-207

图 3-208

图 3-209

图 3-210

图 3-211

图 3-212

图 3-213

2. Breathing Method

Continuing from the previous movement, inhale during the foot landing with passing palm, exhale as you squat down and hold below the waist, inhale while lifting the knee and embracing palms, exhale during the kick with separating palms.

(二)呼吸方法

接上式,落脚穿掌吸气,屈膝下捧呼气,提膝抱掌吸气,蹬脚分掌呼气。

3. Analysis of Power Pathway

Differentiate between solid and empty stances, establish a stable center of gravity before lifting the foot, bend the knee before kicking, and ensure proper support and power generation from the waist and hips.

(三)劲路解析

脚下虚实要分清,独立步要先稳重心再起脚,先屈膝提起再蹬脚,蹬脚时腰胯发力支撑要到位。

4. Examples of Practical Application

Party B strikes Party A's torso with the arms from a distance. Party A's right hand wraps around Party B's hand and grabs the wrist, while the left foot steps forward and the right foot kicks Party B's waist. At the same time, the left hand opens up to maintain balance (Figure 3-214 to 3-217).

(四)实战应用举例

乙方用手臂从远处击打甲方;甲方右手绕乙方手并抓住手腕,左脚上步用右脚蹬踹对方腰部,同时左手展开保持身体平衡。(图 3-214—3-217)

图 3-214

图 3-215

图 3-216

图 3-217

5. Insights on Styles

Techniques are fixed, but people are adaptable. A single technique can have multiple applications, and flexibility and versatility are crucial. As the saying goes, "When resources are scarce, adapt. When adapting, find solutions. When solutions are found, persist." When doing things, people should avoid being overly rigid and learn to think and solve problems using flexible approaches. Being adept at adapting and considering alternative perspectives in daily life is more conducive to problem-solving. We should adhere to a case-by-case analysis, analyze various conditions, and grasp the diversity and conditional nature of relationships.

Ⅲ. Strike to Ears with Both Fists

1.Movement Explanation

(1) Continuing from the previous movement, bend the right knee and retract the foot. Stand on the left foot for support, slightly rotate the body to the right,

(五)招式感悟

招是死的,人是活的,一招多用,灵活多样,懂得变通很重要。所谓:"穷则变,变则通,通则久。是以自天佑之,吉无不利。"人们在做事情的时候不要过分拘泥,应学会运用变通思维去看问题和解决问题。在生活中善于灵活变通,换一种思维方式思考,会更有利于问题的解决。我们要坚持具体问题具体分析,分析各种条件,把握联系的多样性与条件性。

三、双峰贯耳

(一)动作图解

(1)接上式,屈右膝收脚,左脚独立支撑,身体微右转,两掌收于腹前平托,掌心向上(图 3-218)。

and bring both palms to the front of the abdomen, palms facing upward (Figure 3-218).

(2) Step forward to the right front with the right foot, heel touching the ground. Both hands clench into fists and are positioned at the waist (Figure 3-219).

(3) Perform a leg-stretching bow stance. Both fists thrust forward and upward from the sides, reaching forehead height, with the knuckles facing inward (Figure 3-220 and 3-221).

Figure 3-218: Retracting Foot and Supporting Palms

Figure 3-219: Stepping Forward and Clenching Fists

Figure 3-220 and 3-221: Bow Stance and Striking Fists

(2)右脚右前方上步,脚跟着地,两掌握拳收于腰间(图3-219)。

(3)蹬腿弓步,两拳从两侧向前上方贯拳,额头高度,拳眼朝内(图3-220、14-221)。

图3-218 收脚托掌
图3-219 出步握拳
图3-220、3-221 弓步贯拳

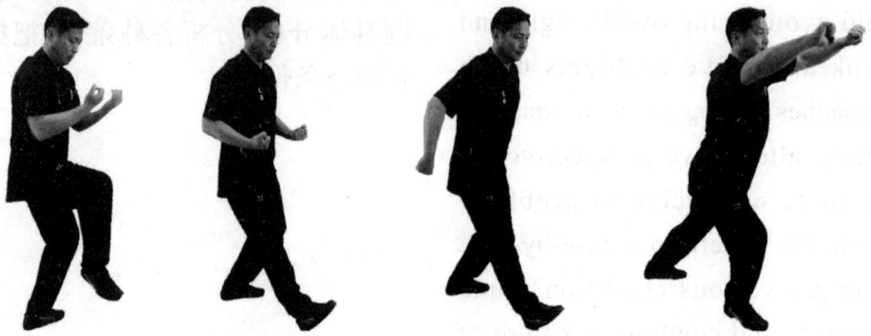

图3–218 图3–219 图3–220 图3–221

2. Breathing Method

Continuing from the previous movement, inhale while retracting the foot and relaxing the palms, exhale during the right rotation and supporting palms, inhale during the stepping forward and clenching fists, exhale during the bow stance and striking fists.

（二）呼吸方法

接上式,收脚松掌吸气,右转托掌呼气,迈步握拳吸气,弓步贯拳呼气。

3. Analysis of Power Pathway

When standing on the supporting foot, maintain a stable center of gravity and loosen the left hip to facilitate the body's right rotation. During the bow stance and penetrating fists, the rear leg pushes forward while the front foot presses down, power is transmitted from the back through the spine to the arms, and the intention reaches the joints of the index fingers.

（三）劲路解析

收脚独立支撑时要稳重心,左侧胯跟松开促进身体右转。弓步贯拳时后腿蹬,前脚踩,力由脊背达于手臂,意达两食指跟节处。

4.Examples of Practical Application

Party B uses both hands to push Party A's torso from the front. Party A grabs Party B's elbow joints and presses down on their arms, clenching both hands into fists and striking Party B's ears from both sides (Figure 3-222 to 3-224).

（四）实战应用举例

乙方用双手从正面推甲方躯干；甲方双手托顶肘关节,翻掌将乙方手臂下按,双手握拳,从两侧击打乙方耳部(图 3-222—3-224)。

图 3-222

图 3-223

图 3-224

5. Insights on Styles

When the palms are insufficient, the fists make up for it. The combined force of the twin fists encompasses the entire body, like a fierce tiger pouncing or giant pincers gripping the face. When the palms are not enough, “favorable winds depend on strength, carrying me to the sky.” We need to understand the value of seeking help and be adept at seeking assistance, leveraging the strength of others. This enables us to attract favorable circumstances and break through the limitations of our individual abilities, moving towards a broader world. We need to learn self-help and also appropriately seek assistance, utilizing various conditions to assist the development of things, achieving quantitative changes that promote qualitative transformations. At the same time, we should concentrate our efforts on important matters and concentrate our main forces on resolving the main contradictions.

（五）招式感悟

掌不够拳来凑，双拳集周身劲，如猛虎扑食，如巨钳夹面。“好风凭借力，送我上青云”。我们要懂得求助、善于求助，善于借助别人的力量，才能引来东风，帮助我们突破个人能力的局限，走向一个更加广阔的世界。我们要学会自助，也要适当善于求助，学会利用各种条件助力事物的发展，量变达到一定程度促进质变。同时要集中力量办大事，集中主要力量解决主要矛盾。

3-6

第七节　转身左蹬脚、左右下势独立

Section 7: Turning and Kicking with Left Heel, and Left-Right Crouch Stance and Beining Lower Body and Golden Rooster Stand

Ⅰ. Turning and Kicking with Left Heel

1.Movement Explanation

(1) Shift the weight backward, raise the tip of the right foot, and turn to the left, separating both fists into palms (Figure 3-225).

(2) Squat down, hands lower and support (Figure 3-226 and 3-227).

(3) Shift the weight to the right, stand on the right foot for support, raise the left leg with a bent knee, cross both hands in front of the chest, with the left hand on the outer side (Figure 3-228).

(4) Kick the left heel to the left side, hooking the tip of the foot. Both palms separate in front of the chest, palm facing forward (Figure 3-229).

Figure 3-225: Retracting Foot and Penetrating Palms

Figure 3-226 and 3-227: Squatting Down and Supporting

Figure 3-228: Lifting Knee and Embracing Palms

Figure 3-229: Kicking the Left Heel and Separating Palms

一、转身左蹬脚

（一）动作图解

（1）重心后移，右脚尖抬起内扣，左转身，两拳变掌分开（图 3-225）。

（2）屈膝下蹲，两手下捧（图 3-226、3-227）。

（3）重心右移，右脚独立支撑，左腿屈膝上提，两手胸前交叉合抱，左手在外侧（图 3-228）。

（4）左脚左侧蹬出，勾脚尖。两掌胸前分掌，立掌，掌心朝前（图 3-229）。

图 3-225 落脚穿掌

图 3-226、3-227 屈膝下捧

图 3-228 提膝抱掌

图 3-229 蹬脚分掌

图 3–225 图 3–226 图 3–227 图 3–228 图 3–229

2. Breathing Method

(二)呼吸方法

Continuing from the previous movement, inhale during the backward shift and left turn, exhale during the squatting down and supporting, inhale during the lifting knee and embracing palms, exhale during the leg thrust and separating palms.

接上式,后移左转吸气,屈膝下捧呼气,提膝抱掌吸气,蹬腿分掌呼气。

3. Analysis of Power Pathway

(三)劲路解析

Distinguish between solidity and emptiness in footwork. When performing the golden rooster stand, ensure stability of the center of gravity before lifting the foot. Bend the knee first and then kick the heel. When kicking the heel, the power generated from the waist and hip should provide strong support.

脚下虚实要分清,独立步要先稳重心再起脚,先屈膝提起再蹬脚,蹬脚时腰胯发力支撑要到位。

4. Examples of Practical Application

(四)实战应用举例

Party B strikes Party A's torso from a distance using their arms. Party A's left hand wraps around Party B's hand and grabs their wrist. Party A steps forward with the right

乙方用手臂从远处击打甲方;甲方左手绕乙方手并抓住手腕,右脚上步用左脚蹬踹对方腰部,同时右手展开保持身体平衡。(图 3-230—3-232)

foot and kicks the left heel to strike Party B's waist, while simultaneously extending the right hand to maintain balance (Figure 3-230 to 3-232).

图 3-230

图 3-231

图 3-232

5. Insights on Styles

Adaptability is one of the indispensable wisdoms for living in this world. When we encounter situations, we need to know how to change our thinking. The world is constantly changing, and trends are constantly evolving. Different situations require different approaches. We should avoid rigidity and dogmatism. " Amidst the mountains and rivers, doubt arises about the path ahead. When the willow is dim, the flowers will shine upon a new village." When we encounter a roadblock in life, we should not get stuck in fixed thinking. Instead, by taking a different route, we may be able to reach our goals. The development of things is not always smooth. The future is bright, but the path is often winding. Progress often occurs amidst twists and turns, resembling a spiral ascent. By learning to adapt, we can

(五)招式感悟

变通是我们活在世上不可或缺的智慧之一,当我们遇到事情时要懂得转变思维。世界本是瞬息万变的,趋势也是不断改变的,不同的情况需要不同的应对方法,做到不死板,不僵化,不教条。"山重水复疑无路,柳暗花明又一村",生活中遇到"此路不通时",不要陷在固有的思维里,而是拐个弯或许就能达到目的。事物的发展不是一帆风顺的,前途是光明的,但道路往往是曲折的,事物的发展往往都是在曲折中前进,呈现螺旋式上升。学会变通,才能处变不惊,才会有更多的可能性。

remain calm in the face of change and open ourselves up to more possibilities.

Ⅱ. Beining Left-Lower Body and Golden Rooster Stand

二、左下式独立

1.Movement Explanation

（一）动作图解

（1）Transitioning from the previous stance, retract the left lower leg by bending the knee. The right palm transforms into a hook with the hook tip facing downward. Place the left palm near the right elbow joint with the palm facing the right arm（the hand position is obscured by the body in the illustration）（Figure 3-233）.

（1）接上式，左小腿屈膝收回，右掌变勾，勾尖朝下，左掌移至右臂肘关节处，掌心对着右臂（图中身体挡住看不到手型）（图3-233）。

（2）Extend the left foot to the left side while bending the right knee to assume a left leaning step. The left palm descends to the front of the abdomen（Figure 3-234）.

（2）左脚左侧伸出，右腿屈膝下蹲成左仆步，左掌下落至腹前（图3-234）。

（3）The back of the left hand is pressed against the inside of the left leg, with the fingertips facing forward along the front of the left leg. Push off with the right leg, shifting the center of gravity forward, and rotate the left foot outward into a left bow stance. The left hand completes the piercing palm movement, while the right hand internally rotates, twists the arm, and the hook tip faces upward behind the body（Figure 3-235 and 3-236）.

（3）左手手背贴着左腿内侧，指尖朝前沿着左腿前穿，蹬右腿重心前移，左脚尖外转成左弓步，左手穿完挑掌，右手内旋拧臂勾尖朝上置于身后（图3-235、3-236）。

（4）The left foot's tip turns outward, shifting the weight forward. The left foot independently supports the body while the right leg is lifted with the knee raised and the toes extended. The left hand descends and rests by the left hip, with the palm

（4）左脚尖外撇，重心前移，左脚独立支撑，收右腿提膝，绷脚尖。左手下落按掌于左胯旁，掌心向下，指尖朝前。右手勾变掌，由下往上挑掌，立掌于右膝上方，掌跟斜向外，指尖鼻尖高度左右（图3-237）。

facing downward and the fingertips pointing forward. The right hand transforms from a hook into a palm, lifting the palm upward from bottom to top and positions it above the right knee, with the heel of the palm slanting outward and the fingertips aligned with the tip of the nose (Figure 3-237).

Figure 3-233: Collecting the Foot and Grabbing with the Hook

Figure 3-234: Stepping to the Left Side

Figure 3-235: Left Leaning Step

Figure 3-236: Step-Through Palm

Figure 3-237: Bow Stance and Lifting Palm

图 3-233 左侧出步

图 3-234 左仆步

图 3-235 仆步穿掌

图 3-236 弓步挑掌

图 3-237 独立立掌

图 3-233

图 3-234

图 3-235

图 3-236

图 3-237

2. Breathing Method

（二）呼吸方法

Following the previous movement, inhale during the foot retraction and hooking, exhale during the left side step, inhale during the step-through palm, exhale during the bow stance and lifting palm, inhale during shifting forward and retracting

接上式，收脚抓勾吸气，左侧出步呼气，仆步穿掌吸气，弓步挑掌呼气，前移收腿吸气，独立按掌呼气。

the leg, and exhale during the golden rooster stand with palms pressing.

3. Analysis of Power Pathway

（三）劲路解析

Transition from a right independent step to a left leaning step, with the right side being substantial and the left side being insubstantial. Shift the center of gravity forward with the left heel as the pivot point, and rotate the left toes outward. The left foot independently supports the body, while the right leg becomes insubstantial and is raised. The left hand should follow the forward shift of the center of gravity and generate energy through the piercing arm movement, while the right hand should first withdraw inward and then push outward, combining the concepts of retracting and extending.

右独立步变左仆步，右实左虚。重心前移左脚跟为轴，左脚尖外转。左脚独立支撑，右腿放虚再上提。左手要随着重心前移做穿臂走劲，右手上提要先回带再向外撑按，有回引再外放之意。

4. Examples of Practical Application

（四）实战应用举例

Crouch Stance and Beining Lower Body: Party B uses the left hand to push Party A's torso from the front. Party A turns to the left and approaches Party B, simultaneously grabbing Party B's left arm with the right hand. The left hand performs a lower body movement through the crotch, while the right hand pulls backward and the left hand lifts upward, flipping Party B from above and throwing them to the ground (Figure 3-238 to 3-242).

仆步下式动作：乙方用左手从正面推甲方躯干；甲方左转身贴近乙方，同时右手抓住乙方左臂，左手左脚下式穿裆，右手后拉，左手上挑，将乙方从上方翻摔倒地。（图3-238—3-242）

Golden Rooster Stand: Party B uses the right arm to push Party A's torso from the front. Party A grabs Party B's right arm with the left hand and pulls Party B's neck inward with the right hand. At the same time, Party A raises the right knee to strike Party B's abdomen or groin area (Figure 3-243 to 3-245).

独立动作：乙方用右臂从正面推甲方躯干；甲方左手拉住乙方右臂，右手抓住对方脖子内收，同时右腿提膝顶击对方腹部或裆部（图 3-243—3-245）。

图 3–238

图 3–239

图 3–240

图 3–241

图 3–242

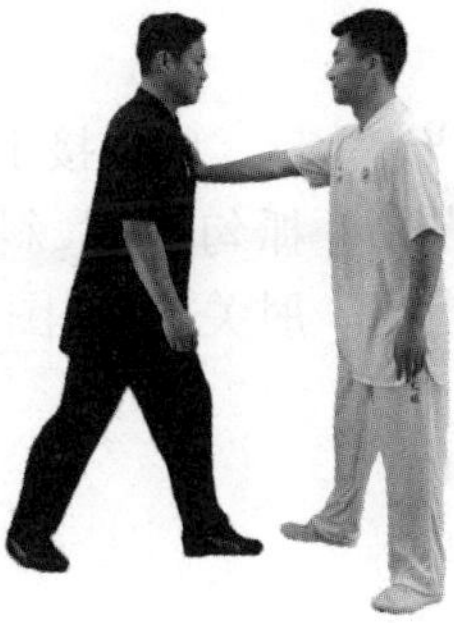

图 3–243

图 3–244

图 3–245

5. Insights on Styles

Excessive force and exaggerated movements should be avoided as they can lead to loss of control. When the opponent suddenly stops resisting, it does not necessarily mean they have conceded; they might be gathering strength. This

（五）招式感悟

力不可太冲，势不可太过，过则容易失势。当对方突然与你不较劲时，不代表对方认输，也可能是在蓄力，厚积薄发。练拳如此，做事亦是如此。凡事要把握适度原则，多一份谨慎，多一份思考。任何事物都有一个界限，要做到张弛有度。任何事物都有两

principle applies not only to martial arts but also to life. We need to maintain a sense of moderation and prudence, carefully considering our actions. Everything has its limits, and we must find a balance between exertion and relaxation. Everything has a dual nature, and we need to adopt a dialectical approach when dealing with problems. We should calmly and comprehensively consider matters, think carefully before acting, be cautious and prudent in our actions, and strive for perfection.

面性，需要我们辩证地看待问题。遇事要冷静全面地思考，三思而后行，做事要小心谨慎，减少麻烦，做到力争完美。

Ⅲ. Beining Right-Lower Body and Golden Rooster Stand

三、右下式独立

1.Movement Explanation

（一）动作图解

(1) Transitioning from the previous stance, turn the body to the left. The right foot touches the ground while the left hand grabs and lifts with a hook, diagonally at shoulder height. The right hand moves and positions the palm to stand on the left elbow joint (Figure 3-246 to 3-248).

（1）接上式，身体左转，右脚点地，左手抓勾提起，斜向肩高，右手移掌立掌于左臂肘关节处（图 3-246—3-248）。

(2) Extend the right foot to the right side while bending the left knee to assume a right leaning step. The right palm descends to the front of the abdomen (Figure 3-249).

（2）右脚右侧伸出，左腿屈膝下蹲成右仆步，右掌下落至腹前（图 3-249）。

(3) The back of the right hand is pressed against the inside of the right leg, with the fingertips facing forward along the front of the right leg. Push off with the left leg, shifting the center of gravity forward, and rotate the right foot outward into a right bow stance. The right hand completes the

（3）右手手背贴着右腿内侧，指尖朝前沿着右腿前穿，蹬左腿重心前移，右脚尖外转成右弓步，右手穿完挑掌，左手内旋拧臂勾尖朝上置于身后（图 3-250、图 3-251）。

piercing palm movement, while the left hand internally rotates, twists the arm, and the hook tip faces upward behind the body (Figure 3-250 and 3-251).

(4) The right foot's tip turns outward, shifting the weight forward. The right foot independently supports the body while the left leg is lifted with the knee raised and the toes extended. The right hand descends and rests by the right hip, with the palm facing downward and the fingertips pointing forward. The left hand transforms from a hook into a palm, lifting the palm upward from bottom to top and positions it above the left knee, with the heel of the palm slanting outward and the fingertips aligned with the tip of the nose (Figure 3-252).

（4）右脚尖外撇，重心前移，右脚独立支撑，收左腿提膝，绷脚尖。右手下落按掌于右胯旁，掌心向下，指尖朝前。左手勾变掌，由下往上挑掌，立掌于左膝上方，掌跟斜向外，指尖鼻尖高度左右（图 3-252）。

Figure 3-246 and 3-247: Turning Left and Grabbing with the Hook

Figure 3-248: Stepping to the Right Side

Figure 3-249: Right Crouch Stance

Figure 3-250: Crouch Stance and Downward Palm

Figure 3-251: Bow Stance and Lifting Palm

Figure 3-252: Golden Rooster Stand with Palm Pressing

图 3-246、3-247 左转抓勾
图 3-248 右侧出步
图 3-249 右仆步
图 3-250 仆步穿掌
图 3-251 弓步挑掌
图 3-252 独立立掌

图 3-246

图 3-247

图 3-248

图 3-249

图 3-250

图 3-251

图 3-252

2. Breathing Method

(二)呼吸方法

Following the previous movement, inhale during the left turn, foot retraction, and hooking, exhale during the right side step, inhale during the crouch stance and downward palm, exhale during the bow stance and lifting palm, inhale during shifting forward and retracting the leg, and exhale during the golden rooster stand with palm pressing.

接上式,左转收脚抓勾吸气,右侧出步呼气,仆步穿掌吸气,弓步挑掌呼气,前移收腿吸气,独立按掌呼气。

3. Analysis of Power Pathway, and Examples of Practical Application

(三)劲路解析、实战应用举例

Please refer to the previous section of "Beining Left-Lower Body and Golden Rooster Stand".

劲路解析、实战应用参考上式"左下式独立"。

4. Insights on Styles

(四)招式感悟

Everything should be done in moderation. Exceeding the limits will lead to a negative outcome, as the saying goes, "The extreme leads to the opposite." The principle of moderation should be upheld in practice,

做任何事情都要有一个度,超过了度,就会走向反面,正所谓"物极必反""过犹不及",在实践中坚持适度的原则,使事物的变化保持在适当的量的范围内,既防止"过",又要防止"不及"。"三思而后行,谋定而后

keeping the variation of things within an appropriate range, avoiding both excess and deficiency. “ Think thrice before acting, plan thoroughly before moving.” It is necessary to approach tasks with caution and careful consideration to prevent unnecessary mistakes during the process.

动”,做事需要有谨慎的态度,需要多一份思考,才能防止在做事过程中出现不必要的错误。

3–7

第八节 左右穿梭、海底针

Section 8: Shuttle Back and Forth, Needle at Sea Bottom

Ⅰ. Shuttle Back and Forth

一、左右穿梭

1.Movement Explanation

(一)动作图解

(1) Transitioning from the previous sequence, the left foot steps forward and to the left, with the heel touching the ground. Both palms relax. The right foot’s heel steps down, and both hands embrace the ball in front of the chest, with the right hand below (Figure 3-253 and 3-254).

(1)接上式,左脚往左前方落步,脚跟先着地,两掌松开。右脚跟步点地,两手胸前抱球,右手在下(图 3-253、3-254)。

(2) The right foot steps forward and to the right, with the heel touching the ground first. The right arm flips the palm and lifts it to the front of the forehead, palm facing outward. The left hand follows the bow stance and pushes forward at chest height (Figure 3-255 and 3-256).

(2)右脚往右前方上步,脚跟先着地。右臂翻掌上提至额头前上方,掌心朝外。左手随弓步前推掌,胸口高度(图 3-255、3-256)。

(3) Shift the weight backward, slightly turn the body to the left, and relax both palms. Shift the weight forward, lift the left foot, and the hands again embrace the ball in front of the chest, with the left hand below (Figure 3-257 and 3-258).

(4) The left foot steps forward and to the left, with the heel touching the ground first. The left arm flips the palm and lifts it to the front of the forehead, palm facing outward. The right hand follows the bow stance and pushes forward at chest height (Figure 3-259 and 3-260).

Figure 3-253: Step Forward to the Left

Figure 3-254: Embrace the Ball with the Right Foot Retracted

Figure 3-255: Step Forward to the Right

Figure 3-256: Push Palm in Bow Stance

Figure 3-257: Shift Backward and Relax Hands

Figure 3-258: Embrace the Ball with the Left Foot Retracted

Figure 3-259: Step Forward to the Left

Figure 3-260: Push Palm in Bow Stance

(3)重心后移,身体微左转,两掌松开。重心前移收左脚点地,两手胸前抱球,左手在下(图3-257、3-258)。

(4)左脚往左前方上步,脚跟先着地。左臂翻掌上提至额头前上方,掌心朝外。右手随弓步前推掌,胸口高度(图3-259、3-260)。

图3-253 左前落步
图3-254 收右脚抱球
图3-255 右前上步
图3-256 弓步推掌
图3-257 后移松手
图3-258 收左脚抱球
图3-259 左前上步
图3-260 弓步推掌

图3–253

图3–254

图3–255

图3–256

图 3-257

图 3-258

图 3-259

图 3-260

2. Breathing Method

（二）呼吸方法

Following the previous movement, inhale during the step forward to the left, exhale while embracing the ball with the right foot retracted, inhale during the step forward to the right, exhale during the push palm in the bow stance, inhale while shifting backward and relaxing the palms, exhale while embracing the ball with the foot in follow step, inhale during the step forward to the left, and exhale during the push palm in the bow stance.

接上式，左前落步吸气，收右脚抱球呼气，右前上步吸气，弓步推掌呼气，后移松掌吸气，跟步抱球呼气，左前上步吸气，弓步推掌呼气。

3. Analysis of Power Pathway

（三）劲路解析

Maintain light and agile footwork, distinguishing clearly between substantial and insubstantial steps. When assuming the bow stance, push off with the rear foot while stepping down with the front foot, ensuring a stable lower body. During the push palm movement, feel the transfer of power from the legs to the waist, back, and then the hands. The upper hand has a sense of supporting and guiding, leading before pushing.

迈步轻盈，脚下虚实分明。弓步时后退蹬前脚踩，下盘沉稳。推掌时体会力由腿及腰背及手地传递，上手有架引之势，引开再推。

4. Examples of Practical Application

（四）实战应用举例

Party B uses the right arm to push against Party A's torso. Party A lifts the left hand upward to redirect Party B's right arm, while using the right palm to strike Party B's abdomen or face (Figure 3-261 to 3-264).

乙方用右臂从正面推击甲方躯干；甲方左手向上将乙方右臂架开，右手用掌击打对方腹部或面部（图 3-261—3-264）。

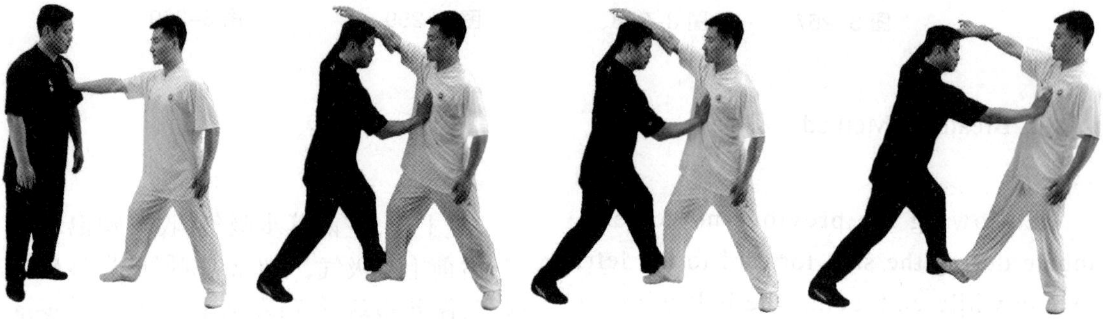

图 3-261 图 3-262 图 3-263 图 3-264

5. Insights on Styles

（五）招式感悟

A successful application of the techniques requires a proper combination of supporting and pushing palms. When the support is properly established, the push becomes effortless. Adequate preparation is necessary to ensure subsequent actions flow smoothly. Tai Chi Chuan utilizes the coordination of spirit, intention, energy, essence, and the movement of the entire body to achieve balance in *qi* and blood, enhance physical strength, and promote the cultivation of a calm and refined mentality.

一架一推掌上功，架引到位，推则轻松。凡事准备工作到位，后续则水到渠成。太极拳在攻防搏击中运用神、意、气、精、劲及周身肢体运动，达到气血阴阳平衡、正气筋力强健，促进心理德性不断淳静、完善、升华，实践实现着中国传统文化中有关致力于献身国家民族“修身、齐家、治国、平天下”的人生观念，激励着一代又一代的有志之士习练太极拳。今天，我们习练太极，强身健体、精进武技，涵养心性，可以更好地服务社会，为国家和民族做出更大的贡献。

It embodies the traditional Chinese cultural concept of "cultivating oneself, harmonizing the family, governing the country, and achieving peace in the world," inspiring generations of aspiring individuals to practice Tai Chi Chuan. Today, by practicing Tai Chi, we can strengthen our bodies, improve martial skills, nurture our minds, and better serve society, making greater contributions to our country and nation.

Ⅱ. Needle at Sea Bottom

1.Movcment Explanation

(1) Transitioning from the previous Sequence, shift the weight forward, half-step with the right foot, and relax both palms (Figure 3-265).

(2) The right foot touches the ground for support, while the left foot remains insubstantial. Rotate the body to the right. The right hand lifts from the right side, upward, while the left hand moves towards the right arm, forming a right-side embrace (Figure 3-266 and 3-267).

(3) Lift the left foot, lower the left hand to the front of the abdomen, bend the right arm to collect the palm, and point the fingertips diagonally downward (Figure 3-268).

(4) Extend the left foot forward, with the toes pointing upward to form an empty step. The left hand arcs to the left and presses the palm on the outside of the left thigh, with the palm facing downward and fingertips pointing forward. The right hand

二、海底针

(一)动作图解

(1)接上式,重心前移,右脚跟半步,两掌放松(图3-265)。

(2)右脚落地支撑,左脚放虚,身体右转,右手从右侧由下往上托,左手往右臂合,做右侧搂手(图3-266、3-267)。

(3)提左脚,左手下落至腹前,右手屈臂收掌,指尖斜向下(图3-268)。

(4)左脚前伸,脚尖虚点成虚步,左手往左画弧按掌于左大腿外侧,掌心向下,指尖朝前。右手前下下插,掌心向内(图3-269)。

moves down and inserts with the palm facing inward（Figure 3-269）.

Figure 3-265：Half-Step with the Right Foot

Figure 3-266 and 3-267：Turn Rightside with Embrace

Figure 3-268：Lift Foot and Retract Palm

Figure 3-269：Insert Palm in Empty Stance

图 3-265 右脚跟步
图 3-266、3-267 右转搂手
图 3-268 提脚收掌
图 3-269 虚步插掌

图 3–265 图 3–266 图 3–267 图 3–268 图 3–269

2. Breathing Method

（二）呼吸方法

Following the previous movement, inhale during Half-step with the Right Foot, exhale during turning rightside with embrace, inhale while lifting the foot and collecting the palm, and exhale during the insert palm in the empty stance.

接上式，后脚跟步吸气，右转搂手呼气，提脚收掌吸气，虚步插掌呼气。

3. Analysis of Power Pathway

（三）劲路解析

The shift of weight should be clear, and the differentiation between substantial

重心转换清晰，虚实分明。腰胯放松，借身体下沉之势做下插掌，主要为上下劲。

and insubstantial should be distinct. Relax the waist and hips, utilizing the sinking momentum of the body to perform the downward insert palm, primarily focusing on the application of upward and downward force.

4. Examples of Practical Application

（四）实战应用举例

Party B grabs Party A's right arm from the front with the left hand. Party A counter-grabs and holds Party B's wrist with the right hand, while pulling both hands to the right and simultaneously swiftly pressing the arms downward, causing Party B to lose balance and fall (Figure 3-270 to 3-273).

乙方用左手从正面拉住甲方右臂；甲方右手反缠并抓住乙方手腕，双手向右侧后拉的同时手臂迅速下按，将乙方失衡倒地。（图 3-270—3-273）

图 3–270

图 3–271

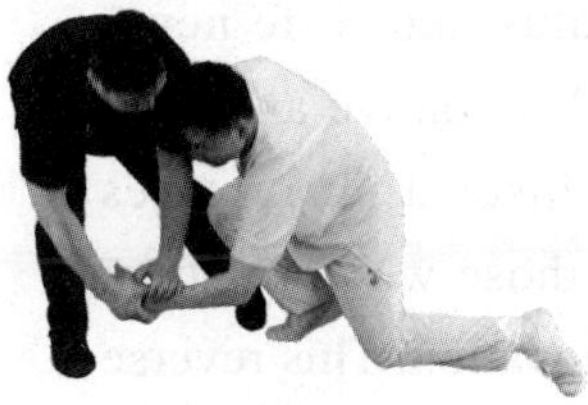

图 3–272

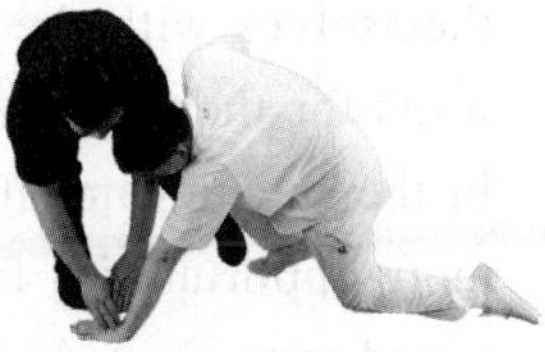

图 3–273

5. Insights on Styles

（五）招式感悟

One up, one down; one lead, one hang. To hang, first lead; to capture, give slack. The approach of Tai Chi Chuan is based on the principle of selflessness, adaptability, and responsiveness, and it showcases the functional aspects of martial techniques. In a state of relaxation and

一上一下，一引一挂。欲挂先引，欲擒故纵。太极拳的对待因应之道是采取舍己从人、因应随顺的法则发挥技击对待的功能。在松静自然的状态下，以自身本体的感觉，通过感官的直觉与身体的接触而获得对方动静各方面的信息，并且在瞬间加以处理，达到彼不动，己不动，彼微动，己先

naturalness, one relies on the sensations of their own body, utilizing intuitive perception and physical contact to gather information about the opponent's movements and intentions. In an instant, this information is processed to achieve control: not moving when the opponent doesn't move, moving first when the opponent makes subtle movements. "The wise adapt themselves to circumstances; the knowledgeable shape the world accordingly." "To solve deep-seated contradictions and problems, the fundamental path lies in innovation." Only those who innovate can advance, only those who innovate can be strong, only those who innovate can prevail. Life never favors those who adhere to old ways and content themselves with the status quo. Life never waits for those who lack initiative and bask in their achievements. Instead, it reserves more opportunities for those who are adept at and courageous in innovation. This reverse philosophical thinking applies not only to martial arts but also to life and work.

动的掌控能力。"明者因时而变,知者随世而制""解决深层次矛盾和问题,根本出路在于创新",唯创新者进,唯创新者强,唯创新者胜;生活从不眷顾因循守旧、满足现状者,从不等待不思进取、坐享其成者,而是将更多机遇留给善于和勇于创新的人。这种反向哲学思维不仅适用于拳术中,也适用于生活和工作中。

3–8

第九节 闪通臂、转身搬拦捶

Section 9: Flashing the Arm and Turning Body to Deflect Downward, Parry and Punch

Ⅰ. Flashing the Arm

1.Movement Explanation

(1) Transitioning from the previous stance, bring back the left foot, lift the right palm upward with the palm facing left, and raise the left palm to the right wrist with the palm facing right (Figure 3-274 and 3-275).

(2) Step forward with the left foot, rotate the body to the right, flip the right palm and place it above the forehead at a slanting angle, with the palm facing outward (Figure 3-276).

(3) Extend the right leg to form a left bow step and push forward with the left palm (Figure 3-277).

一、闪通臂

（一）动作图解

（1）接上式，左脚回收，右掌上提，掌心向左，左掌提至右手腕处，掌心向右（图3-274、3-275）。

（2）左脚往前上步，身体右转，右手翻掌上架至额前斜上方，掌心向外（图3-276）。

（3）蹬右腿成左弓步，左掌向前推掌（图3-277）。

图 3–274

图 3–275

图 3–276

图 3–277

Figure 3-274 and 3-275: Bring Back Foot and Lift Hand

Figure 3-276: Step Forward and Place Palm Above

Figure 3-277: Bow Stance and Push Palm

图 3-274、3-275 收脚提手
图 3-276 上步架掌
图 3-277 弓步推掌

2. Breathing Method

（二）呼吸方法

Following the previous movement, inhale while lifting the foot and flipping the palm, and exhale during the push with the bow step.

接上式，提脚迈步翻掌吸气，弓步推掌呼气。

3. Analysis of Power Pathway

（三）劲路解析

The flipping of the right palm and placing it above involve the transfer of force through the body's rotation. The waist and hips should be relaxed to facilitate the rotation. The pushing force of the left palm is supported by the grounding of the right leg and the solid positioning of the left foot, creating coordination between the left palm and the right leg on the same side.

右手翻掌架引由身体右转发力引带，此时腰胯要放松，利于旋转。左手推掌力由右腿的蹬地、左脚的踩实，左掌和右腿在同一面上形成呼应。

4. Examples of Practical Application

（四）实战应用举例

Party B pushes Party A's torso forward using the right hand from the front. Party A responds by lifting Party B's right arm upward, stepping forward with the left foot, and using the left palm, fist, or elbow to strike the right side of Party B's torso (Figure 3-278 to 3-282).

乙方用右手从正面推甲方躯干；甲方用右手将乙方右臂向上架开，左脚上步，用左手掌或拳或肘击打乙方右侧躯干。（图3-278—3-282）

图 3-278

图 3-279

图 3-280

图 3-281

图 3-282

5. Insights on Styles

Evading the body, placing the palm above, and pushing straight forward, exploiting weaknesses with flexible strikes. Various parts of the body coordinate and penetrate each other, achieving perfect interaction between the main and the subordinate, just like the operation of Tai Chi, where the main contains the subordinate and the subordinate contains the main, integrating the main and the subordinate. It is important to establish a sense of the overall situation, be skilled in examining problems from a broad perspective, look at the world and the future; be adept at observing the general trend and planning significant matters, and grasp the initiative in work. This requires both a decisive and resolute style and the calmness of taking a leisurely stroll. It is necessary to learn to observe and handle problems from a strategic and global perspective, perceive the essence and laws of development through the complex surface phenomena, and achieve a balance between focusing on key issues and overall considerations, as well as balancing current

（五）招式感悟

闪身架引直掌推，避实就虚击软肋。身体各部位彼此配合，互渗互入，主客之间达于完美的整体互动，如太极之运行，主中有客，客中有主，主客合一。要树立大局意识，善于从大局看问题，放眼世界，放眼未来；善于观大势、谋大事，把握工作主动权；既有雷厉风行的作风，也有闲庭信步的定力。要学会站在战略和全局的高度观察和处理问题，透过纷繁复杂的表面现象把握事物的本质和发展的规律，做到既抓住重点又统筹兼顾，既立足当前又放眼长远。此种道化之境即是艺道一体的太极人生之意义。寻得法门，方得巧妙。

actions and future prospects. This state of philosophical understanding represents the significance of the integration of art and the Tao in the Tai Chi way of life. Discovering the method is the key to achieving mastery.

Ⅱ. Turning Body to Deflect Downward, Parry and Punch

二、转身搬拦捶

1.Movement Explanation

（一）动作图解

（1）Shift the weight backward, inwardly turn the left foot, rotate the body to the right, and relax both palms（Figure 3-283 and 3-284）.

（2）Transfer the weight to the left foot, lift the right foot, and move the left palm in an arc to the front of the chest, horizontally across the chest with the palm facing downward. The right palm transitions into a fist and descends to the front of the abdomen with the back of the fist facing forward（Figure 3-285）.

（3）Lower the right foot forward, the heel touching the ground, forming an empty step. The right fist moves from the inner side of the left hand, lifting upward and forward, with the back of the fist facing forward（Figure 3-286 and 3-287）.

（4）Rotate the body to the right, pivot the right foot accordingly to support the stance, bring the right fist to the waist, and move the left palm to the left side of the body（Figure 3-288 and 3-289）.

（5）Lift the left foot and step forward, the left palm intercepts and presses in front of the body（Figure 3-290）.

（1）重心后移，左脚内扣，身体右转，两掌放松（图 3-283、3-284）。

（2）重心移至左脚，右脚提起，左掌画弧移至胸前，横于胸前，掌心向下，右掌变拳下落至腹前，拳背朝前（图 3-285）。

（3）右脚前落，脚跟着地成虚步，右拳从左手内侧由下往上、往前搬拳，拳背朝前（图 3-286、3-287）。

（4）身体右转，右脚顺势拧转落脚支撑，右拳立拳收于腰间，左掌移至身体左侧（图 3-288、3-289）。

（5）提左脚向前迈步，左掌拦按于体前（图 3-290）。

（6）Push off with the back leg to form a left bow step, the right fist punches forward, assuming a fist position, while the left palm is pressed against the right elbow joint, assuming an upright palm position with the palm facing right（Figure 3-291）.

（6）后腿蹬地成左弓步，右拳向前冲拳，立拳，左掌收按于右臂肘关节处，立掌，掌心向右（图 3-291）。

Figure 3-283：Shifting Weight Backward

Figure 3-284：

Figure 3-285：Lifting Foot and Clenching Fist

Figure 3-286 and 3-287：Empty Stance and Move Fist

Figure 3-288 and 3-289：Right Turn and Retracting Fist

Figure 3-290：Stepping Forward and Intercepting Palm

Figure 3-291：Bow Stance and Punch Fist

图 3-283 重心后移
图 3-284 扣脚右转
图 3-285 提脚握拳
图 3-286、3-287 虚步搬拳
图 3-288、3-289 右转收拳
图 3-290 上步拦掌
图 3-291 弓步冲拳

图 3-283

图 3-284

图 3-285

图 3-286

图 3-287

图 3-288

图 3-289

图 3-290

图 3-291

2. Breathing Method

Transitioning from the previous sequence, inhale during the inward turn of the foot and rotation, exhale during the empty step and moving fist, inhale when stepping forward and intercepting palm, and exhaling during bowing stance and punching fist.

（二）呼吸方法

接上式，扣脚右转吸气，虚步搬拳呼气，上步拦掌吸气，弓步打拳呼气。

3. Analysis of Power Pathway

This movement consists of three parts: moving fist, intercepting palm, and punching. When performing the moving fist, the left palm has the intention of leading and pressing, while the right fist uses the elbow joint as an axis to twist the arm and press or strike. During the intercepting palm, the left palm presses down with the intention of sealing and covering. When executing the punch, it is necessary to combine the force of leg thrust and the power of the waist and hips.

（三）劲路解析

此式由搬拳、拦掌、冲拳三个部分组成，搬拳时左掌有引按封住之意，右拳以肘关节为轴拧臂翻按或翻打；拦掌时左掌按住，有封盖之意；冲拳时要结合蹬腿及腰胯的力量。

4. Examples of Practical Application

Deflecting Downward: Party B pushes Party A's torso forward from the front using the right hand. Party A responds by pressing down Party B's arm with the left hand, delivering a fist strike to Party B's facial area from the inside to the outside, while the tip of the right foot hooks tightly, the heel descends, striking Party B's lower leg, and then stepping down on Party B's foot. At the same time, both hands exert force to push forward, causing Party B to fall to the ground(Figure 3-292 to 3-298).

Parrying and Punching: Party B pushes Party A's torso forward from the front using the right hand. Party A's left hand pushes Party B's arm to the right side, while the right hand delivers a fist strike to Party B's abdomen or ribs(Figure 3-299 to 3-301).

（四）实战应用举例

搬动作：乙方用右手从正面推甲方躯干；甲方左手下按乙方手臂，右手由内向外用拳击打对方面部，右脚脚尖勾紧、脚跟向下，踹击对方小腿，随后向下踩踏对方脚部，同时双手发力前推，使乙方落空倒地（图3-292—3-298）。

拦捶动作：乙方用右手从正面推甲方躯干；甲方左手将乙方手臂向右侧推出，同时右手用拳击打对方腹部或肋部（图3-299—3-301）。

图 3-292

图 3-293

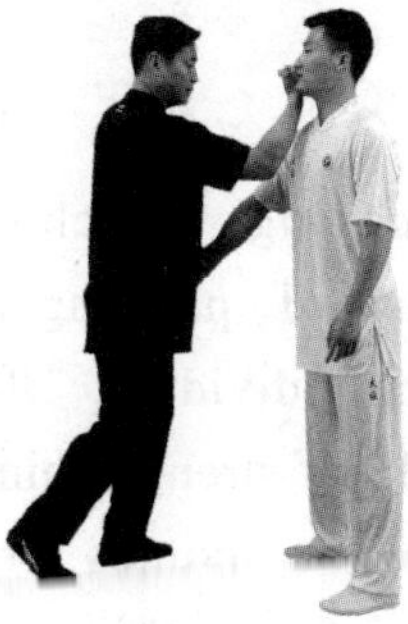

图 3-294

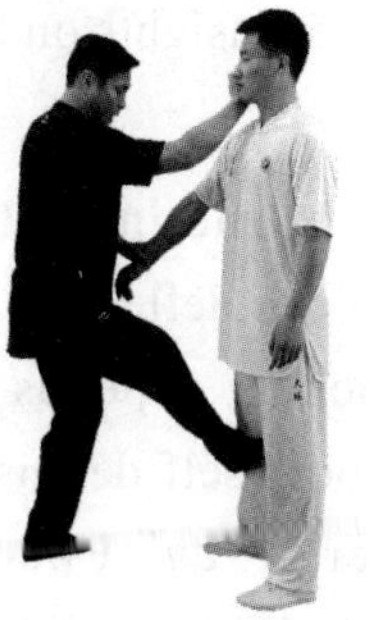

图 3-295

图 3-296

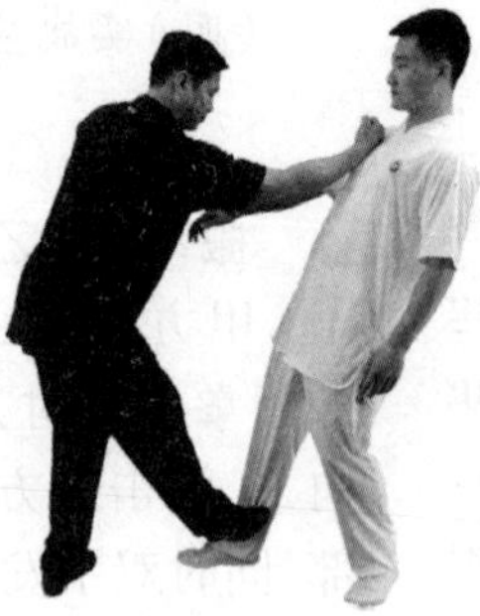

图 3-297

图 3-298

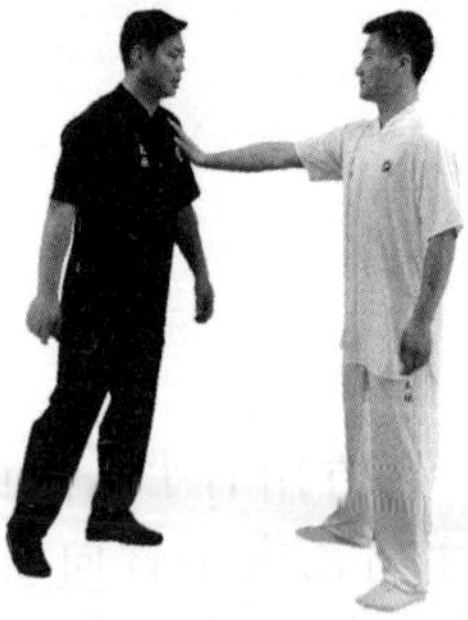

图 3-299

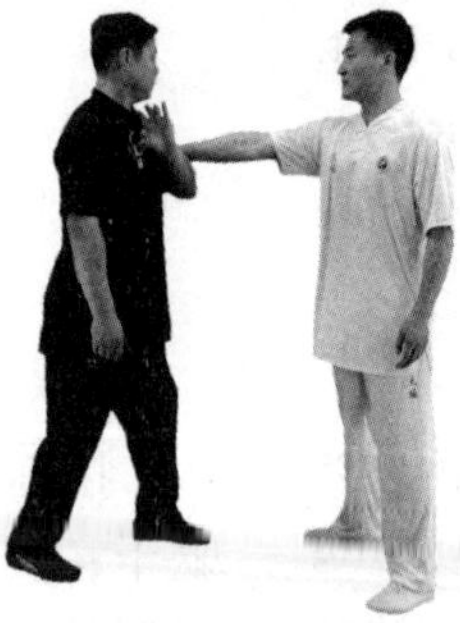

图 3-300

图 3-301

5. Insights on Styles

In the instant of moving, the choice between deflecting downward, parrying and punching depends on the individual. "*Wu*" is about self-defense and self-strengthening, where "*ren*" (benevolence) comes first. Techniques can be used for pushing and self-defense can involve striking. Tai Chi requires the involvement of the whole body, wholeheartedness, and the completion of a single breath. The flow of Tai Chi involves the unity of the self and the fist, remaining calm and smooth, facilitating movements from the heart, and achieving a harmonious integration, like the operation of Tai Chi,

（五）招式感悟

搬拦推打一瞬间，是推是打个人选。"武"乃强身自卫，"仁"字当先，较技可推，自卫可打。太极拳要求全身参与，全心投入，完整一气，太极拳的行运是拳我合一，沉着顺遂，便利从心，圆融一体，如太极的运行，圆满和谐。我们要培养辩证思维能力，具体问题具体分析，善于抓住事物主要矛盾和矛盾的主要方面，更加全面准确地认识和把握事物，做到透过现象看本质。

achieving completeness and harmony. We need to develop the ability for dialectical thinking, analyzing specific problems in a specific manner, being adept at grasping the main contradictions and the primary aspects of contradictions, and achieving a more comprehensive and accurate understanding and grasp of things, seeing through the surface to the essence.

3-9

第十节　如封似闭、十字手、收势

Section 10：Apparent Close up，Cross Hands，and Closing Form

Ⅰ. Apparent Close up

一、如封似闭

1.Movement Explanation

（一）动作图解

（1）Continuing from the previous sequence，move the left hand below the right arm with the palm facing upward，slide forward along the right arm，transforming the right fist into an open palm. Both palms separate and are shoulder-width apart，with the palms facing upward（Figure 302 to 3-304）.

（2）Shift the weight back，sitting on the rear leg，flex both arms and draw them back to the front of the chest，fingertips facing upward. Then，flip the palms and press downward to the front of the abdomen，fingertips facing forward（Figure 3-305 and 3-306）.

（1）接上式，左手移至右臂下方，掌心向上，沿着右臂往前平抹，右拳变掌，两掌分开与肩宽相当，两掌心朝上（图 3-302—3-304）。

（2）蹬前腿重心后坐，两掌屈臂向胸前回收，指尖朝上，随后翻掌下按至腹前，指尖朝前（图 3-305、3-306）。

(3) Both hands arc upward to chest height, while pushing forward with a bow step (Figure 3-307 and 3-308).

(3)双手弧线上提至胸口高度,蹬腿弓步往前推掌(图 3-307、3-308)。

Figure 3-302: Sliding Palm
Figure 3-303: Separating Palms
Figure 3-304: Palms Up
Figure 3-305: Flexing Palms
Figure 3-306: Flipping Palms
Figure 3-307 and 3-308: Pushing Palms

图 3-302 抹掌
图 3-303 分掌
图 3-304 掌心向上
图 3-305 收掌
图 3-306 翻掌
图 3-307、3-308 推掌

图 302

图 3–303

图 3–304

图 3–305

图 3–306

图 3–307

图 3–308

2. Breathing Method

(二)呼吸方法

Continuing from the previous sequence, inhale during the sliding palms and separating palms, and exhale during the lifting hands and pushing palms.

接上式,抹手分掌回收吸气,提手推掌呼气。

3. Analysis of Power Pathway

（三）劲路解析

The movement relies on leg thrust to shift the center of gravity and promote forward power through the body. During the downward press and retreat, it is important to tuck in the abdomen and flex the hips without leaning backward. When pushing the palms forward, use leg thrust and hip force to propel forward, with the front foot acting as a brake. The body should not lean forward excessively or violate the principle of stability.

重心移动靠腿蹬，以身促手力前行。后引下按时要收腹屈胯，不可后仰。前推掌时要蹬腿顶胯力前送，前脚踩住起制动，身不可前俯犯冲。

4. Examples of Practical Application

（四）实战应用举例

Party B pushes Party A's torso forward from the front using both hands. Party A supports the elbows with both hands, shifts the weight backward, and then flips both hands, pressing down Party B's arms to the abdomen. Party B resists with force from behind, and Party A leverages the force to push Party B forward, causing Party B to lose balance and fall to the ground (Figure 3-309 to 3-312).

乙方用双手从正面推甲方躯干；甲方双手上托肘关节，后移重心，随后两手翻掌将对方手臂下按到腹部，乙方向后用力对抗，甲方借力向前发力将乙方推出，使乙方落空倒地(图 3-309—3-312)。

图 3-309

图 3-310

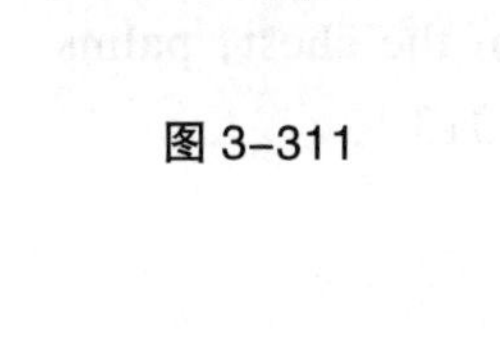

图 3-311

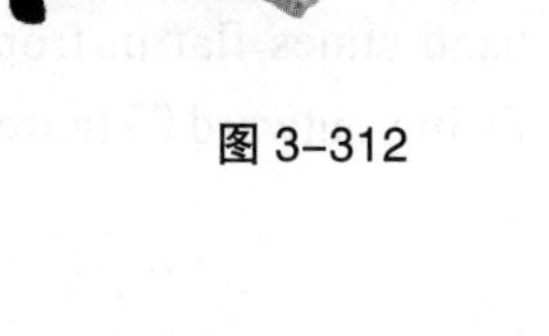

图 3-312

5. Insights on Styles

One pull, one release; one retreat, one throw; like surging waves with hidden currents. The throw is only the result, while the skill lies in the art of leading before the throw. It's similar to how the visible outcome of a person's hard work is often apparent, but the process of the hard work is often unknown to others. In reality, the process of effort is the essence, and the result is just the ultimate manifestation. In life and work, we should adopt a dialectical perspective, not only seeing the contradictions and opposition between the two sides but also recognizing their unity. We should see both the favorable and unfavorable aspects, as well as our own strengths and the difficulties and problems we face. We need to study dialectics diligently, comprehensively, systematically, and accurately grasp the fundamental principles, links, and laws of connection and development, and consciously apply them in our thinking.

(五)招式感悟

一引一放,一回一掷,如波涛汹涌,暗流涌动。掷放只是结果,掷前的引才是巧妙之处。这就像一个人努力的结果往往是显而易见的,但努力的过程往往不被人所知,其实努力的过程才是努力的主体,结果只是终极表现而已。生活和工作中,我们要用辩证的观点看问题,不仅要看到矛盾双方的对立,而且要看到矛盾双方的统一,既看到有利的一面,也看到不利的一面;既看到自身的优势,也看到面临的困难和问题。要认真学习辩证法,全面、系统、准确地掌握联系和发展的基本观点、基本环节和基本规律,将其自觉地体现和运用于思维当中。

Ⅱ. Cross Hands, Closing Form

二、十字手、收势

1.Movement Explanation

(1) Continuing from the previous sequence, shift the weight to the right, turning the body to the right. Lift the left toe inward and the right toe outward. The right hand slides flat in front of the chest, palms facing outward (Figure 3-313).

(一)动作图解

(1)接上式,重心右移,蹬左腿右转身,左脚尖抬起内扣,右脚尖抬起外撇,右手在胸前平抹拉开,两掌立掌,掌心向外(图3-313)。

(2) Squat down with bent knees, lower both hands, and hold them down (Figure 3-314).

(2)屈膝下蹲,两手下落,下捧(图3-314)。

(3) Step back with the right foot and bring it together, crossing both hands in front of the chest, with the right hand on the outside (Figure 3-315).

(3)右脚蹬地顺势收半步,两手捧起至胸前交叉合抱,右手在外侧(图3-315)。

(4) Internally rotate both arms and open the palms with a rolling motion, palms facing downward, shoulder-width apart (Figure 3-316).

(4)两臂内旋滚动平抹掌打开,掌心向下,肩宽左右(图3-316)。

(5) Apply downward force with the palms to the front of the abdomen, then relax the hands by the sides of the body, and rise up by pushing with the legs (Figure 3-317 and 3-318).

(5)沉劲按掌至腹前,随后两手松于体侧,蹬腿起身(图3-317、3-318)。

(6) Lift the left foot and step forward (Figure 3-319).

(6)提左脚并步(图3-319)。

Figure 3-313: Turning with Separating Palms

Figure 3-314: Squatting and Holding Down

Figure 3-315: Crossing and Holding

Figure 3-316: Flipping and Sliding Palms

Figure 3-317: Applying Downward Force with Palms

Figure 3-318: Relaxing Hands and Rising Up

Figure 3-319: Lifting Foot and Stepping Forward

图3-313 右转分掌
图3-314 屈膝下捧
图3-315 收脚合抱
图3-316 翻转抹掌
图3-317 沉劲按掌
图3-318 松手起身
图3-319 提脚并步

图 3–313

图 3–314

图 3–315

图 3–316

图 3–317

图 3–318

图 3–319

2. Breathing Method

Continuing from the previous sequence, inhale during the turning with separating palms, exhale during the squatting and holding down, inhale during the flipping and sliding palms, exhale during the applying downward force with palms, inhale during the rising up and lifting foot, and exhale during the foot landing and stepping.

3. Analysis of Power Pathway

During the turning with separating palms, shift the weight to the right side. During the squatting and holding down, shift the weight to the left side. When flipping and sliding palms in the cross hands position, there should be a rolling and twisting movement in the forearms. During the downward palm press, sink the energy to the soles of the feet and the *qi* to the *dantian*. Return to the original position, achieve calmness, and restore the stance.

（二）呼吸方法

接上式，右转分掌吸气，下捧收脚呼气，翻转抹掌吸气，沉劲按掌呼气，起身提脚吸气，落脚并步呼气。

（三）劲路解析

右转分掌时重心往右侧偏移，下捧收脚时重心再往左侧偏移。十字手翻转平抹时两前臂需有滚动拧转之意，下按掌时要随着劲往脚底沉，气往丹田沉的势做下按。一切收于原始，归于平静，并步还原。

4. Examples of Practical Application

（四）实战应用举例

Application of Cross Hands: Party B grabs Party A from the front with both hands. Party A simultaneously crosses and draws in both hands, clamping Party B's arms at the armpits, and crossing hands to support Party B's elbow joints, creating a clamp. Party A uses the legs to push upward, throwing Party B off balance, kneeing the groin, or striking the opponent's face with the head (Figure 3-320 to 3-322).

Application of Closing Form: Party B grabs Party A's arm and attempts a back throw. Party A slightly bends the knees, simultaneously pulls the hands back and downward, causing Party B to lose balance and fall (Figure 3-323 to 3-325).

十字手用法：乙方从正面用双手抱住甲方；甲方两手同时交叉内收下抱，同时在腋部夹住对方双臂，双手交叉托顶对方肘关节，形成钳制，双脚用力向上蹬地、将乙方甩倒或提膝顶裆或用头撞击对方面部（图3-320—3-322）。

收势用法：乙方拉住甲方手臂进行背摔；甲方微微屈膝下蹲，同时双手向后回收并且下拉，使乙方落空倒地（图3-323—3-325）。

图 3–320

图 3–321

图 3–322

图 3–323

图 3–324

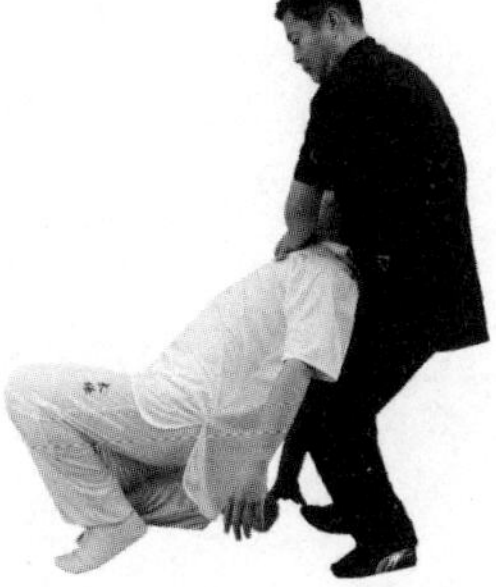

图 3–325

5. Insights on Styles

To truly understand Tai Chi, one must embrace its principles and actively practice with a dedicated attitude. Tai Chi is not just a physical activity but a holistic practice of body, mind, and spirit, rooted in the philosophy of practical dialectics. Practicing Tai Chi is about understanding the universe and enriching one's life. The process of skill cultivation often starts with rough movements and gradually refines them, from large to small, from external to internal, mutually complementary. It involves three cycles of transformation until sudden enlightenment and understanding are reached. This practice is gradual and progressive, requiring continuous advancement and perseverance. When mastery is achieved, the movements become subtle, and clarity and understanding arise.

(五)招式感悟

对于太极拳的体认,要以皈依于太极的性理,积极的实践修炼态度来加以认识太极拳,太极拳不只是一种体育活动,更是身心灵一体修炼且富有实践辩证的力行哲学。练太极拳就是在认识宇宙与充实人生。技艺的修炼过程往往是由粗而精,由大而微,由外而内,互为表里,三回九转,最后豁然已解。此一实践过程是渐修、渐长,境界的提升是拾级而上,盈科而进,非一蹴可及,达到纯熟时,动之甚微,豁然开朗,豁然而解。

3–10

第四章　中国大学生太极推手竞赛规则

Chapter 4: Rules of the Chinese University Students Tai Chi Push Hands Competition

第一节　太极实战推手通则

Section 1: General Regulations for Tai Chi Practical Push Hands

Article 1: Nature of the Competition

1. Individual Competition
2. Team Competition

Article 2: Competition Methods

1. Round-Robin: Single Round-Robin, Group Round-Robin
2. Elimination: Single Elimination, Double Elimination

Article 3: Eligibility and Examination of Participants

1. Participating athletes must be officially enrolled students with regular student status at national ordinary higher education institutions (including junior college, undergraduate, graduate, and

第一条 竞赛性质

1. 个人赛
2. 团体赛

第二条 竞赛办法

1. 循环赛：单循环、分组循环
2. 淘汰赛：单败淘汰、双败淘汰

第三条 参赛资格及审查

1. 参赛运动员必须具有全国普通高等院校(含大专、本科、研究生、留学生)正式学籍学生。参赛运动员必须携带身份证及学生证。

international students). Participants must carry their identification card and student ID.

2. Athletes must provide proof of personal insurance coverage for participating in the competition.

3. Athletes must present a valid physical examination certificate issued by a county-level or higher hospital within 15 days prior to the registration date, including indicators such as electroencephalogram, electrocardiogram, blood pressure, and pulse.

2. 运动员必须提供参加该次比赛的人身保险证明。

3. 运动员必须出示报到之日前 15 天内，县级及以上医院出具的包括脑电图、心电图、血压、脉搏等指标在内的体格检查合格证明。

Article 4：Weight Categories

48 kg weight category (≤ 48 kg)
52 kg weight category (>48 kg– ≤ 52 kg)
56 kg weight category (>52 kg– ≤ 56 kg)
60 kg weight category (>56 kg– ≤ 60 kg)
65 kg weight category (>60 kg– ≤ 65 kg)
70 kg weight category (>65 kg– ≤ 70 kg)
75 kg weight category (>70 kg– ≤ 75 kg)
80 kg weight category (>75 kg– ≤ 80 kg)
85 kg weight category (>80 kg– ≤ 85 kg)
Above 85 kg weight category (>85 kg)

第四条 体重分级

48 公斤级(≤ 48Kg)
52 公斤级(>48Kg —≤ 52kg)
56 公斤级(>52Kg —≤ 56kg)
60 公斤级(>56Kg —≤ 60kg)
65 公斤级(>60Kg —≤ 65kg)
70 公斤级(>65Kg —≤ 70kg)
75 公斤级(>70Kg —≤ 75kg)
80 公斤级(>75Kg —≤ 80kg)
85 公斤级(>80Kg —≤ 85kg)
85 公斤级以上级(>85Kg)

Article 5：Weigh-In

1. Weigh-in is conducted before the draw.

2. Athletes can participate in the weigh-in only after passing the eligibility examination and must carry their identification card and student ID.

3. Weigh-in must be conducted under the supervision of the arbitration committee, led by the check-in chief, and assisted by the recording officer.

4. Athletes must weigh in according to the designated time and location specified by the conference. During the weigh-in, athletes should only wear shorts (female athletes may wear tight-fitting undergarments).

5. Weigh-in starts from the lowest weight category set for the competition, with each category being weighed within 30 minutes. If the weight does not match the registered category or if the athlete fails to reach the registered weight category within the designated weigh-in time, they will not be allowed to participate in any subsequent matches.

第五条 称量体重

1. 称量体重在抽签前进行。

2. 运动员经资格审查合格后方可参加称量体重,并且必须携带身份证及学生证。

3. 必须在仲裁委员的监督下称量体重,由检录长负责,编排记录员配合完成。

4. 运动员必须按照大会规定的时间到指定地点称量体重。称量体重时只穿短裤(女子运动员可穿紧身内衣)。

5. 称量体重先从比赛设定的最小级别开始,每个级别在30分钟内称完。如体重不符,在规定的称量时间内达不到报名级别时,则不准参加后面所有场次的比赛。

Article 6: Drawing Lots

1. Drawing lots takes place after the weigh-in, starting from the lowest weight category set for the competition. If there is only one person in that category, they cannot participate in the competition.

2. The drawing of lots is the responsibility of the scheduling and recording team, and is attended by the Director or members of the Arbitration Committee, the Vice Chief

第六条 抽签

1. 称量体重后进行抽签,由比赛设定的最小级别开始。如该级别只有1人,则不能参加比赛。

2. 由编排记录组负责抽签,由仲裁委员会主任或委员、副总裁判长及参赛队的教练或领队参加。

Referee, and the coaches or team leaders of the participating teams.

Article 7: Competition Time

第七条 竞赛时间

Each match is divided into two rounds, with each round lasting 1 minute and 30 seconds of hand-pushing. During the break between rounds, the athletes exchange positions before the next competition.

每场比赛分为两局,每局净推 1 分 30 秒,局间双方运动员交换场地继续比赛。

Article 8 : Competition Signals

第八条 竞赛信号

1. Ten seconds before the start of the match, the timekeeper blows the whistle to indicate readiness. At 1 minute and 30 seconds into each round, the timekeeper sounds the gong to announce the end of the round.

1. 比赛前 10 秒钟,计时员鸣哨通告准备;每局比赛至 1 分 30 秒,计时员鸣锣宣告该局比赛结束。

2. On the field, referees use verbal commands and gestures to make judgments during the competition.

2. 场上裁判员用口令和手势裁定比赛。

Article 9 : Forfeiture

第九条 弃权

1. During the competition, if an athlete is unable to participate due to injury or illness, they must provide a certificate from the conference doctor to declare a forfeiture.

1. 比赛期间,运动员因伤病不宜参加比赛时,须有大会医生证明,作弃权论。

2. Athletes who fail to check-in three times or leave after checking-in are considered forfeits.

2. 三次检录未到,或检录后自行离开者作弃权论。

3. During the competition, athletes can raise their hand to request a forfeiture, and coaches can also throw a white towel to request a forfeiture to the on-field referee.

3. 比赛过程中,运动员可举手要求弃权,教练员也可向场上裁判员扔白毛巾要求弃权,运动员自己终止比赛,作弃权论。

If an athlete terminates the match by themselves, it is considered a forfeiture.

4. If an athlete forfeits the competition without a valid reason, all their results for that competition will be canceled.

4. 比赛期间,运动员无故弃权,取消本人在此比赛中的全部成绩。

Article 10: Competition Etiquette

第十条 竞赛礼仪

1. "Referees' Entry Ceremony": Referees enter the field and stand in a straight line facing the arena in front of the Chief Referee's seat. When introducing the referees, they should stand upright and bow to the audience.

1. "裁判员入场式": 裁判员入场,站在裁判长席前方,面向擂台一字排开。介绍裁判员时,裁判员应该成立正姿势向观众行抱拳礼。

2. "Athletes' Entry Ceremony": Before the entry of all participating athletes, they line up in order of their categories, from small to large. Under the guidance of the staff, they enter the field, with the black and white teams standing on both sides of the arena, facing the arena. When the command "Bow" is given, all athletes bow with half of their bodies towards all referees. When the command "Athletes bow to each other" is given, the athletes from the black and white teams face each other and bow.

2. "运动员入场式":所有参赛运动员入场前按照级别由小到大的顺序站成一路纵队。入场时在工作人员带领下分黑白两方列于擂台两侧,面向擂台。宣告给出"行礼"口令时,所有运动员侧半身与所有裁判员互行抱拳礼,出现"运动员相互行礼"口令时,黑白两列运动员面对面互行抱拳礼。

3. After the athletes step onto the arena, they stand on both sides of the on-field referee, facing the Chief Referee. When introducing an athlete, the person being introduced should first bow to the Chief Referee in a proper manner, and then bow to the audience.

3. 运动员上擂台后,站在场上裁判员两侧,面向裁判长。介绍运动员时,被介绍者应呈立正姿势先向裁判长行抱拳礼,再向观众行抱拳礼。

4. After the introduction of both athletes is completed, they bow to each other and then bow to the on-field referees.

5. At the end of each match, after the on-field referee announces the result of the match, the athletes first bow to the referee, then bow to each other, and finally turn around to bow to the opposing coach before exiting the field.

4. 在双方运动员介绍结束后,运动员互行抱拳礼,再与场上裁判员互行抱拳礼。

5. 每场比赛结束时,运动员在场上裁判员宣布比赛结果后,先向裁判员行抱拳礼,然后相互行抱拳礼,再转身向对方教练员行抱拳礼,方可退场。

Article 11: Competition Attire

第十一条 竞赛服装

Athletes must participate in the competition wearing the Tai Chi Push Hands professional competition attire designated by the Chinese Wushu Association.

运动员必须着中国武术协会指定的太极推手专业竞赛服装参加比赛。

Article 12 : Competition Regulations

第十二条 竞赛相关规定

1. Athletes must abide by the competition rules, compete earnestly, and deliberate injury is strictly prohibited.

2. Coaches and team doctors should sit in designated areas and refrain from making loud noises or shouting during the competition.

3. Athletes are not allowed to request a pause during the competition. In case of special circumstances, they must raise their hand to signal the on-field referee.

4. Athletes are not allowed to have long nails, wear wristwatches, or bring items that are easily damaged or may cause harm to opponents onto the competition field.

1. 运动员必须遵守比赛规则,认真进行比赛,严禁故意伤人。

2. 教练员和本队医生应坐在指定位置,比赛时不得在场下大声喧哗、呼喊。

3. 比赛时运动员不得要求暂停,如遇特殊情况,需向场上裁判员举手示意。

4. 运动员不可留长指甲、不可戴腕表和易伤及对方的物品上场比赛。

第二节　太极实战推手裁判人员及其职责

Section 2: Referees and Their Responsibilities in Tai Chi Practical Push Hands

Article 13：Composition of Referees

1. Main Referees

Chief Referee：1 person；Deputy Chief Referees：1-2 persons

Referee-in-Chief and Deputy Referee-in-Chief：1 person each

On-Field Referee：1 person；Side Referees：3-5 persons

Recorder and Timekeeper：1 person each

Scheduling and Recording Chief：1 person

Check-in Supervisor：1 person

2. Assistant Referees

Scheduling and Recording Assistants：2-3 persons

Check-in Officials：2-3 persons

Announcers：1-2 persons

Medical Personnel：2-3 persons

Electronic Scoring System Operators：1-2 persons

第十三条 裁判人员的组成

1. 执行裁判

总裁判长 1 人，副总裁判长 1 ～ 2 人。

裁判长、副裁判长各 1 人。

场上裁判员 1 人，边裁判员 3 ～ 5 人。

记录员、计时员各 1 人。

编排记录长 1 人。

检录长 1 人。

2. 辅助裁判

编排记录员 2 ～ 3 人。

检录员 2 ～ 3 人。

宣告员 1 ～ 2 人。

医务人员 2 ～ 3 人。

电子计分系统操作员 1 ～ 2 人。

Article 14: Responsibilities of Referees

1. Chief Referee

Organizes referee training on competition rules, procedures, and explains the referee regulations.

Is responsible for assigning tasks to the referee team.

Resolves competition-related issues based on the spirit of the competition regulations and rules, but has no authority to modify the competition rules and procedures.

Guides the work of the referee team during the competition and has the authority to adjust the referees' assignments. In case of disputes in the referee's work, has the authority to make the final decision.

Organizes the chief referee's inspection before the competition to ensure the implementation of the venue, equipment, and relevant referee equipment.

2. Deputy Chief Referee

Assists the chief referee's work and can assume their responsibilities in their absence.

3. Referee-in-Chief

Is responsible for the learning and work arrangements of the referees in their group.

Supervises and guides the work of the referees, timekeepers, and recorders during the competition.

Whistles to indicate correction when an on-field referee makes an obvious misjudgment or omission.

With the consent of the chief referee, the side referees can change their judgment

第十四条 裁判人员的职责

1. 总裁判长

组织裁判员学习竞赛规则、规程，讲解裁判法。

负责裁判组的分工。

根据竞赛规程和规则的精神，解决竞赛中的有关问题，但无权修改竞赛规则和规程。

比赛中指导裁判组的工作，有权调动裁判员的工作。在裁判工作有争议时，有权作出最后决定。

赛前组织裁判长检查落实场地、器材和有关裁判用具。

2. 副总裁判长

协助总裁判长工作，总裁判长缺席时可代行其职责。

3. 裁判长

负责本组裁判员的学习和工作安排。

比赛中监督和指导裁判员、计时员、记录员的工作。

场上裁判员有明显错判、漏判时，鸣哨提示改正。

边裁判员出现明显错判，宣布结果前征

if they make an obvious misjudgment before announcing the result.

得总裁判长同意后可以改判。

Handles matters related to advantage, penalties, mandatory counting, based on the on-site athlete's situation and the recorder's records.

根据临场运动员的情况和记录员的记录,处理优势胜利、处罚、强制读秒等有关规定事宜。

Announces the judging result and determines the winner after each match.

每场比赛结束后,宣布评判结果,决定胜负。

4. Deputy Referee-in-Chief

4. 副裁判长

Assists the referee-in-chief's work and can also serve as other referees as needed.

协助裁判长工作,根据需要可以兼任其他裁判员的工作。

5. On-Field Referee

5. 场上裁判员

Conducts safety checks on the on-field athletes and promptly corrects any non-compliance with the rules to ensure the safety of the competition.

对临场运动员进行安全检查,如发现有与规则不符者,应及时纠正,保障比赛安全进行。

Commands the athletes using verbal commands and gestures during the match.

用口令和手势指挥运动员进行比赛。

Determines matters such as athletes falling, leaving the stage, committing fouls, displaying passivity, mandatory counting, on-site treatment, etc.

判定运动员倒地、下台、犯规、消极、强制读秒、临场治疗等有关事宜。

Announces the result of each match.

宣布每场比赛结果。

6. Side Referees

6. 边裁判员

Determine the scores of the athletes based on the rules.

根据规则判定运动员的得分。

After receiving the signal from the referee-in-chief, simultaneously and promptly display the judging results.

每场比赛结束后,根据裁判长信号,同时、迅速显示评判结果。

Sign and keep the scoring sheets after each match for verification.

每场比赛结束后,在计分表上签名并保存,以备检查核实。

7. Recorder

7. 记录员

Fills in the relevant information in the record sheet carefully before the match.

赛前认真将有关信息填入记录表。

Participates in weighing the athletes and records their weights in the record sheet for each match.

参加称量体重的工作，并将每名运动员的体重填入每场比赛的记录表。

Based on the commands and gestures of the on-field referees, records the number of warnings, advisories, mandatory counting, and stage exits for the athletes.

根据场上裁判员的口令和手势，记录运动员被警告、劝告、强制读秒、下台的次数。

Records the judging results of each side referee and reports them to the referee-in-chief after determining the winner.

记录边裁判员每场的评判结果，确定胜负后报告裁判长。

8. Timekeeper

8. 计时员

Checks the gong, timer, and approves the stopwatch before the match.

赛前检查铜锣、计时器，核准秒表。

Is responsible for timing during the match, pauses, and mandatory counting.

负责比赛、暂停、读秒的计时。

Whistles to announce the start of each game, 10 seconds before each game.

每局比赛前 10 秒钟鸣哨通告。

Announces the end of each game by sounding the gong.

每局比赛结束鸣锣通告。

In the absence of an electronic scoring system, announces the side referees' judging results at the end of each game.

无电子计分系统的情况下，每局比赛结束时，宣读边裁判员的评判结果。

9. Scheduling and Recording Chief

9. 编排记录长

Is responsible for athlete qualification review and examination of registration forms.

负责运动员资格审查，审核报名表。

Is responsible for organizing the drawing of lots and arranging the order of matches for each game.

负责组织抽签，编排每场比赛秩序表。

Prepares various forms required for the competition and verifies and records the results.

预备竞赛中所需要的各种表格；审查核实成绩，录取名次。

Registers and announces the results of each match.

登记和公布每场比赛成绩。

Compiles a scorebook by collecting and summarizing relevant data.

统计和收集有关资料，汇编成绩册。

10. Scheduling and Recording Assistants

Carry out tasks assigned by the scheduling and recording chief.

11. Check-in Supervisor

Is responsible for weighing the athletes.

Inspects and manages the competition attire.

Calls the athletes for check-in 30 minutes before the match.

In case of issues such as athletes not showing up or forfeiting during check-in, promptly reports to the chief referee.

Inspects the athletes' attire, nails, and accessories according to the requirements of the rules.

12. Check-in Officials

Carry out tasks assigned by the check-in supervisor.

13. Announcers

Provide a brief introduction to the competition regulations, rules, and relevant promotional materials.

Introduce the on-field referees and athletes.

Announce the judging results.

14. Medical Personnel

Review the athletes' Physical Examination Forms.

Conduct random medical examinations of athletes before the competition.

Provide on-site injury treatment and management.

10. 编排记录员

根据编排记录长分配的任务进行工作。

11. 检录长

负责称量运动员的体重。

负责竞赛服装的检查和管理。

赛前30分钟负责召集运动员检录。

检录时,如出现运动员不到或弃权等问题,及时报告裁判长。

按照规则的要求,检查运动员的服装和指甲、饰品。

12. 检录员

根据检录长分配的任务进行工作。

13. 宣告员

简要介绍竞赛规程、规则和有关的宣传材料。

介绍临场裁判员、运动员。

宣告评判结果。

14. 医务人员

审核运动员的"体格检查表"。

负责赛前对运动员进行体检抽查。

负责临场伤病的治疗与处理。

Assess injuries caused by fouls.

负责因犯规造成运动员受伤情况的鉴定。

Supervise medical matters during the competition. If an athlete is unfit to continue the competition due to injury or illness, promptly recommend their withdrawal to the chief referee.

负责竞赛中的医务监督,对因伤病不宜参加比赛者,应及时向裁判长提出 其停赛建议。

Cooperate with doping control personnel to check whether athletes have used prohibited substances.

配合兴奋剂检测人员检查运动员是否使用违禁药物。

Article 15: Electronic Scoring System Operator

第十五条 电子计分系统操作员

Responsible for tasks related to the operation of the electronic scoring system.

负责与电子计分系统操作相关的工作。

第三节 太极实战推手仲裁委员会及其职责与申诉

Section 3: Tai Chi Push Hands Arbitration Committee and Its Responsibilities and Appeals

Article 16: Composition of the Arbitration Committee

第十六条 仲裁委员会的组成

The Arbitration Committee consists of a director, deputy director, and 3 or 5 members.

由主任、副主任,以及其他3到5个成员组成。

Article 17: Responsibilities of the Arbitration Committee

第十七条 仲裁委员会的职责

The Arbitration Committee works under the leadership of the conference. Its main responsibility is to handle appeals from participating teams regarding disputes or

仲裁委员会在大会的领导下进行工作。主要受理参赛队对裁判员有关违反竞赛 规程、规则的判决结果有不同意见的申诉。

disagreements with the referees' decisions that violate the competition regulations and rules.

It accepts appeals from participating teams regarding objections to the referees' decisions in executing the competition regulations and rules, limited to appeals concerning their own team's decisions.

Upon receiving an appeal, it should be processed immediately without delaying other matches, ranking assessments, and prize distribution. Once a decision is made, the relevant participating teams should be notified promptly.

Based on the circumstances presented in the appeal materials, if necessary, video reviews and investigations can be conducted. The Arbitration Committee convened for discussions and studies. Relevant personnel may be invited to attend the meeting without voting rights. The decision of the Arbitration Committee requires a majority of attendance for validity. In the case of equal voting results, the director of the Arbitration Committee has the final decision-making authority.

Members of the Arbitration Committee shall not participate in discussions regarding issues that involve their own affiliated teams.

After a thorough and serious review of the raised appeal issues, if it is confirmed that the original decision was correct, the original decision shall be upheld. If it is confirmed that there was a clear error in the original decision, the Arbitration Committee shall submit a request to the Chinese Wushu Association for handling the

受理参赛队对裁判执行竞赛规程、规则的判决结果有异议的申诉,但只限对本 队判决的申诉。

接到申诉后,应立即进行处理,不得延误其他场次的比赛、名次的评定及发奖。裁决出来后,应及时通知有关参赛队。

根据申诉材料提出的情况,必要时可以复审录像,进行调查。召开仲裁委员会 讨论研究。开会时可以邀请有关人员列席参加,但无表决权。仲裁委员会出席人数必须超过半数以上做出的决定方为有效。表决结果相等时,仲裁委员会主任有终裁权。

仲裁委员会成员不参加本人所在单位参赛队有牵连问题的讨论。

对申诉提出的问题,经过严肃认真复审,确认原判无误,则维持原判;如确认原判有明显错误,仲裁委员会提请中国武术协会对错判的裁判员按有关规定处理,但不改变评判结果,仲裁委员会的裁决为最终裁决。

referee responsible for the incorrect decision according to relevant regulations, but the judgment result shall not be changed. The decision of the Arbitration Committee shall be final.

Article 18: Appeal Procedure and Requirements

If a sports team disagrees with the decision of the referee group, they must submit a written appeal to the Arbitration Committee within 15 minutes after the completion of the athlete's match, accompanied by an appeal fee of 1000 yuan. If the appeal is deemed valid, the appeal fee shall be refunded while upholding the original decision. If the appeal is deemed invalid, the original decision shall be upheld and the appeal fee shall not be refunded.

All teams must abide by the final decision of the Arbitration Committee. If there is unreasonable harassment, depending on the severity of the situation, it may be recommended for serious actions to be taken by the Competition Supervision Committee or the Organizing Committee.

第十八条 申诉程序及要求

运动队如果对裁判组的裁决结果有异议,必须在该运动员比赛结束后 15 分钟内,由本队领队或教练向仲裁委员会提出书面申诉,同时交付 1000 元的申诉费。如申诉正确,退回申诉费,但维持原判;申诉不正确的,维持原判,申诉费不退。

各队必须服从仲裁委员会的最终裁决。如果无理纠缠,根据情节轻重,可以建议竞赛监督委员会、组委会给予严肃处理。

第四节　太极实战推手竞赛监督委员会及其职责

Section 4: Tai Chi Push Hands Competition Supervision Committee and Its Responsibilities

Article 19: Composition of the Competition Supervision Committee

To supervise the work of the Arbitration Committee. Criticize, educate, replace, or even suspend individuals who fail to fulfill their responsibilities of the Arbitration Committee, render unfair judgments on appeals from sports teams, or violate the "*Arbitration Committee Regulations*," depending on the severity of the situation.

To supervise the work of referees. Criticize, educate, replace, suspend, or recommend disciplinary actions such as demotion or revocation of referee status for individuals who fail to fulfill their responsibilities, fail to conduct refereeing in a serious, diligent, fair, and accurate manner, exhibit clear violations of regulations and rules, make obvious errors and omissions, or biased judgments, accept bribes from sports teams, or show favoritism towards athletes, depending on the severity of the situation.

To supervise the behavior of team leaders, coaches, and athletes from participating units. Apply criticism, education, notifications, cancellation of competition results, and

第十九条 竞赛监督委员会的组成

监督仲裁委员会的工作。对于不能正确履行仲裁委员会职责，判决运动队的申诉不公正，有违反《仲裁委员会条例》的人员，视情节轻重，给予批评、教育、撤换乃至停止工作的处分。

监督裁判人员的工作。对于不能正确履行自己的职责，不能严肃、认真、公正、准确地进行裁判，有明显违反规程、规则的行为者，有明显错判、漏判的行为者，接受运动队贿赂，以不正当的手段偏袒运动员者，视情节轻重，给予批评、教育、撤换、停止工作，乃至建议对其实施降级或撤销其裁判等级的处分。

监督参赛单位各领队、教练、运动员的行为。对于不遵守《赛区工作条例》《运动员守则》，不遵守竞赛规程、规则及赛场纪律，对参赛队行贿，运动员之间搞交易、打假

disqualification from the competition to individuals who do not comply with the "*Competition Area Regulations*," "*Athlete Code of Conduct*," violate competition regulations, rules, and field discipline, engage in bribery within participating teams, or participate in fraudulent matches and other disciplinary violations, depending on the severity of the situation.

赛等有关违纪人员,视情节轻重,给予批评、教育、通报、取消比赛成绩、取消比赛资格等处分。

The Competition Supervision Committee listens to feedback and opinions from team leaders, coaches, athletes, arbitrators, and referees regarding various aspects of the competition process to ensure a fair, accurate, successful, and smooth competition.

竞赛监督委员会听取领队、教练、运动员、仲裁人员、裁判人员对竞赛过程中的各种反映及意见,保证竞赛公正、准确、圆满、顺利地进行。

The Competition Supervision Committee does not directly engage in the responsibilities within the scope of the Arbitration Committee and referees' duties. It does not interfere with the proper fulfillment of duties by the Arbitration Committee and referees, intervene in disputes over judgment results, or change the decisions of the referee group and the Arbitration Committee.

竞赛监督委员会不直接参与仲裁委员会、裁判人员职责范围内的工作,不干涉仲裁委员会、裁判人员正确履行自己的职责,不介入判决结果的纠纷,不改变裁判组的裁决结果和仲裁委员会的裁决结果。

第五节 太极实战推手技法要求、得分标准与判罚

Section 5: Requirements of Tai Chi Push Hands Techniques, Scoring Criteria, and Penalties

Article 20: Competition Rules

The "*peng* (warding off), *lv* (rolling back), *ji* (pressing), *an* (pushing), *cai* (pulling down), *lie* (splitting), *zhou* (elbowing), *kao* (body stroke)" elements (referred to as the eight techniques) and corresponding footwork must be used.

The principles of "adhering, sticking, connecting, and following" and "combining softness and hardness" must be implemented.

第二十条 竞赛法则

必须采用“掤、捋、挤、按、採、挒、肘、靠”的方法元素(简称八法),以及相应的步法。

必须贯彻“沾粘连随”“刚柔相济”的原则。

Article 21: Competition Methods

1. Tai Chi Push Hands Individual

(1) When the referees give the command "prepare," the athletes from both sides assume the starting position and make contact with each other. In the first round, the white side leads, and in the second round, the black side leads.

(2) At the beginning of the first round, both sides have their right foot forward and interlock their right hands. After switching sides in the second round, both sides have their left foot forward and interlock their left hands.

(3) At the start of each round, the front foot of both athletes is placed within the

第二十一条 竞赛方法

1. 太极实战推手个人部分

(1)当场上裁判员发出“预备”口令时,双方运动员起势、上步成合步搭手势。第一局白方领手,第二局黑方领手。

(2)第一局开始时,双方右脚在前,互搭右手;第二局互换场地后,双方左脚在前,互搭左手。

(3)每局开始时,双方运动员前脚踩于中心圈内,合步搭手,当场上裁判员发出开

central circle, and they interlock their hands. Once the referees give the starting signal, the match begins.

始信号后,比赛开始。

(4) During the match, athletes can freely move their front foot within the circle and their rear foot within their own area.

(4)比赛过程中,运动员前脚可以在圈内任意移动,后脚可以在本方区域内任意移动。

(5) During the match, both athletes can change footwork, but the following three situations are not allowed:

(5)比赛过程中,双方运动员可以进行步法变换,但不能出现以下三种情况:

1) Both feet stepping simultaneously on the centerline.

1)运动员双脚同时踩到中线。

2) Both feet crossing the centerline simultaneously.

2)运动员双脚同时超过中线。

3) One foot stepping on the centerline while the other foot steps into the opponent's area.

3)运动员一只脚踩住中线,另一只脚过中线踩在对手的区域内。

(6) If both athletes lose contact during the match without the referees calling a stop, they can directly resume the attack when they regain contact.

(6)比赛过程中,双方脱手,场裁未喊停的情况下,双方搭手,可直接进攻。

(7) When the referees call a stop and give the command "interlock hands," both athletes must return to the center point and interlock their hands.

(7)比赛过程中,当场上裁判员喊停,并发出"搭手"口令时,双方运动员需回到中心点搭手。

(8) After the match ends, under the guidance of the referees on the field, athletes stand on both sides of the referees and await the announcement of the match results.

(8)比赛结束后,在场上裁判的指示下,运动员站在裁判员两侧等待宣布比赛结果。

2. Tai Chi Push Hands Team

(1) The team competition is divided into three weight categories: lightweight (below 65 kg, including 65 kg), middleweight (65 kg to 80 kg, including 80 kg), and heavyweight (above 80 kg).

(2) Each team selects three athletes for each weight category (can choose one category). Each athlete competes in one round, with a net pushing time of 1 minute and 30 seconds. The first team to score three points wins. If the time ends with both teams having equal scores below three points, the match continues until one team scores. The winning team earns one point, while the losing team does not receive any points. The team with the highest total score ranks higher.

2. 太极实战推手团体部分

(1)团体赛分三个公斤组,轻量组(65 kg 以下,包含 65 kg)、中量组(65 kg 至 80 kg,包含 80 kg)、重量组(80 kg 以上)。

(2)每队每组别(可任选一组别)报 3 人,每人打一局,净推 1 分 30 秒,一方率先得三分者获胜。若时间结束,双方分数相等且低于 3 分,则继续比赛,率先得分者胜。获胜总分加 1 分,失败不加分。团体总分高者,名次列前。

Article 22: Target Areas for Attacks

The trunk and arm regions below the neck and above the pubic bone.

第二十二条 攻击部位

颈部以下,耻骨以上之躯干和手臂部位。

Article 23: Prohibited Target Areas

Areas above the neck, including the neck itself.

Areas below the pubic bone, including the pubic bone.

第二十三条 禁击部位

颈部及颈部以上部位。

耻骨及耻骨以下部位。

Article 24：Passive Competition

When athletes do not initiate an attack for 5 seconds during the match，the referee on the stage must designate one athlete from the passive side or either side of the passive participants to initiate an attack. The referee on the stage designates one athlete to attack and counts to 5 by using hand gestures at a rate of one count per second. If the athlete fails to initiate an attack within 5 seconds，the referee shall call "stop" and penalize the designated side with "passive competition."

第二十四条 消极比赛

比赛中运动员互不进攻时间达 5 秒时，台上裁判员须指定消极一方运动员或双方消极中的任何一方进攻。台上裁判员指定一方运动员进攻后，按每秒一次的频率用手指在体侧记数 5 次的方法计时，运动员达 5 秒钟仍不进攻时应喊"停"，并给予被指定方"消极比赛"的判罚。

Article 25：Scoring

1. Victory by Advantage

(1) If an injury caused by the opponent's foul prevents an athlete from continuing the match，the injured athlete is declared the winner.

(2) If an athlete is unable to continue the match due to injury (except for injuries caused by the opponent's foul)，the opponent is declared the winner.

(3) If an athlete or coach requests to forfeit，the opponent is declared the winner.

(4) When the point difference between the two athletes reaches 15 points，the athlete with the higher score is declared the winner.

(5) If the same athlete is forced to take two countdowns，the match is terminated，and the opponent is declared the winner.

(6) If the same athlete steps off the platform twice，the opponent is declared the winner.

第二十五条 得分

1. 优势胜利

（1）比赛中因对方犯规造成受伤，经医生检查不能继续比赛者，判受伤者获胜。

（2）比赛中因受伤（除因对方犯规而致的受伤外）不能坚持比赛者，判对方获胜。

（3）比赛中运动员或教练员要求弃权时，判对方获胜。

（4）双方运动员分差达到 15 分时，判得分高者优势获胜。

（5）一场比赛中，同一运动员被强制读秒两次，则终止比赛，判对方获胜。

（6）一场比赛中，同一运动员下擂两次，判对方获胜。

(7) If one side accumulates 4 penalty points, the opponent is declared the winner.

2. 3 Points

(1) If one side falls to the ground (any part of the body except for supporting contact with the ground), the standing opponent earns 3 points.

(2) If one side steps off the platform, the opponent earns 3 points.

3. 2 Points

(1) If the opponent is forced to touch the ground with one hand (including supporting contact), 2 points are awarded.

(2) If one side steps on or goes outside the designated circle, the opponent earns 2 points.

(3) If one side is forced to take a countdown, the opponent earns 2 points.

(4) If one side receives a warning, the opponent earns 2 points.

(5) For violations listed in Rule 7 of the "Offensive Foul," a warning is given, and the opponent earns 2 points.

4. 1 Point

(1) For violations listed in Rules 1-6 of the "Offensive Foul," a caution is given, and the opponent earns 1 point.

(2) For violations listed in the "Technical Foul," a caution is given, and the opponent earns 1 point.

(3) If one side steps on or goes inside the inner circle, the opponent earns 1 point.

(4) If one side steps with the trailing foot or crosses the centerline, the opponent

（7）一场比赛中，一方受罚达 4 分时，判对方获胜。

2. 得 3 分

（1）一方倒地（除附加支撑外，任何部位接触地面均为倒地），对方站立者得 3 分。

（2）一方下擂，对方得 3 分。

3. 得 2 分

（1）凡使对方单手接触地面（附加支撑）者，得 2 分。

（2）一方踩踏或出外圈者，对方得 2 分。

（3）一方被强制读秒一次，对方得 2 分。

（4）一方受警告一次，对方得 2 分。

（5）凡出现“侵人犯规”中的第 7 条者，给予警告，对方得 2 分。

4. 得 1 分

（1）凡出现“侵人犯规”中的 1 ~ 6 条之一者，给予劝告，对方得 1 分。

（2）凡出现“技术犯规”之一者，给予劝告，对方得 1 分。

（3）一方脚踩踏或出内圈者，对方得 1 分。

（4）一方后脚踩踏或过中心线者，对方得 1 分。

earns 1 point.

(5) If a participant is penalized with "passive competition," the opponent earns 1 point.

(5) 被判消极比赛者,对方得1分。

5. No Points

(1) When both sides step off the platform or fall to the ground simultaneously.

(2) Invalid attacks.

(3) Attacks that do not utilize the "eight techniques" elements.

5. 不得分

(1) 双方同时出圈或倒地。

(2) 无效进攻。

(3) 凡不使用"八法"技术元素进攻对方者。

Article 26: Fouls

第二十六条 犯规

1. Offensive Fouls

(1) Using forceful pulling, dragging, embracing, or using foot hooks, stomps, trips, or kneeling.

(2) Intentionally causing the opponent to commit a foul.

(3) Releasing forceful strikes or collisions.

(4) Grabbing or tightly holding the opponent's clothing.

(5) Initiating an attack before the command "begin" or after the command "stop."

(6) Using hands to attack the pubic bone or areas below it.

(7) Performing actions such as punching, headbutting, thrusting arms, seizing, grabbing hair, acupoint striking, elbow striking, crotch digging, leg sweeping, knee striking, or choking.

1. 侵人犯规

(1) 使用硬拉、硬拖、搂抱,或用脚勾、踩、绊、跪者。

(2) 故意造成对方犯规者。

(3) 脱手发力击、撞者。

(4) 抓握对方衣服或死握对方者。

(5) 在口令"开始"前或喊"停"后进攻对方者。

(6) 用手攻击对方耻骨及耻骨以下部位者。

(7) 使用拳打、头撞、撅臂、擒拿、抓头发、点穴、肘尖顶、捞裆、扫腿、膝撞、扼喉等动作者。

2. Technical Fouls

(1) Being impolite or disobedient to the referee during the match.

(2) Raising a hand to request a pause while in a disadvantaged position.

3. Penalties

(1) For each occurrence of Offensive Fouls 1–6, a caution is given.

(2) For each occurrence of Offensive Foul 7, a warning is given.

(3) For each occurrence of Technical Foul, a caution is given.

(4) In a match, if the same athlete receives two warnings or accumulates 8 penalty points, the match is terminated, and the opponent is declared the winner.

(5) Athletes intentionally causing harm will be disqualified from the competition.

Article 27: Ranking Evaluation

1. After the completion of the competition, the victory or defeat of each match is determined based on the judgment of the sideline referees.

2. In the event of a draw, the following principles shall be followed:

(1) The lighter athlete is declared the winner.

(2) If the weights are still equal, the athlete with fewer warnings is declared the winner.

(3) If the warnings are still equal, the athlete with fewer admonitions is declared the winner.

(4) Overtime will be conducted, and the athlete who scores first will be declared

2. 技术犯规

(1)比赛中对裁判员不礼貌或不服从裁判者。

(2)处于不利状况时举手要求暂停者。

3. 处罚规则

(1)出现“侵人犯规”1 ~ 6条之一,每犯规一次,判劝告一次。

(2)出现“侵人犯规”第7条,每犯规一次,判警告一次。

(3)技术犯规一次,判劝告一次。

(4)一场比赛中,同一运动员被警告两次或者被罚分达8分者,则终止比赛,判对方获胜。

(5)运动员故意伤人者,取消比赛资格。

第二十七条 评定名次

1. 比赛结束后,依据边裁判员的判罚结果,判定每场比赛胜负。

2. 出现平局时,按下列原则处理

(1)体重轻者为胜方。

(2)如仍相等,以警告少者为胜方。

(3)如仍相等,以劝告少者为胜方。

(4)进行加时赛,先得分者为胜方。

the winner.

Article 28: Technical Specifications

第二十八条 技术规范

Contact: The wrists of both parties make contact, with the forearms forming an arc. The point of contact is at the centerline between both parties, and the wrists are level with the chin. The other hand is attached to the opponent's elbow.

搭手：双方腕部接触，前臂呈弧形。触点在双方中线，腕部与下颌齐高。另一手附于对方肘部。

Issuing Force: Force must be applied after the hands make contact with the opponent.

发放：必须在手接触到对方后发力。

第六节 太极实战推手裁判员的口令和手势图解

Section 6: Verbal Instructions and Gestures for Tai Chi Push Hands Referees

Article 29: Verbal Instructions and Gestures for Competition Etiquette and General Penalties

第二十九条 有关竞赛礼节与一般判罚的口令和手势

1. Salute: Stand with legs together, with the left palm and right fist clasped in front of the chest at the same level, with a gap of 20–30 centimeters between the fist and the chest.

1. 抱拳礼：双腿并步站立，左掌右拳胸前相抱，高与胸齐，拳与胸之间间隔为20~30厘米。

2. Athletes Enter: The referee enters the field first, and the on-field referee stands in the center of the field with palms facing upwards, pointing straight ahead towards the

2. 比赛进场：裁判员首先进场，场上裁判员站在场地中心，两掌心向上直臂指向双方运动员，在发出“运动员进场”口令的同时，两手屈臂上举，掌心朝内。

athletes. At the command "Athletes Enter," both hands are bent upwards, with palms facing inward.

3. Prepare—Begin: The on-field referee stands in the middle of the athletes with arms extended, palms facing upwards, pointing towards the athletes. The command "Prepare" is given, followed by clasping the hands together and pressing downwards, while simultaneously issuing the command "Begin."

3. 预备—开始：场上裁判员站在双方运动员中间，两臂伸直仰掌指向双方运 动员，发出"预备"口令，随即向内合掌并下按，同时发出"开始"口令。

4. Start of Each Game: Take a step forward with the right foot, and extend the right hand with the index finger extended for the first game, and the index and middle fingers extended for the second game.

4. 每局开始：向前右弓步，右手向前伸出食指为第一局，伸出食指和中指为第二局。

5. Exchange Field: Stand upright with legs together, arms extended straight with palms facing inward, and cross them below the body.

5. 交换场地：两腿并拢直立，两臂伸直掌心向内，于体前下方交叉。

6. Stop: The on-field referee extends one arm toward the middle of the athletes and simultaneously gives the command "Stop," indicating a pause in the match.

6. "停"：场上裁判员一臂伸向运动员中间，同时发出"停"的口令，比赛即为暂停。

7. One Side Falls: The on-field referee points one arm towards the side that falls first, and while giving the command "One Side Falls," the other arm presses downward in front of the body, palms facing down.

7. 一方倒地：场上裁判员一臂指向先倒地一方，在发出"某方倒地"口令的 同时，另一臂在体前下按，掌心朝下。

8. Fall First: The on-field referee points one arm towards the side that falls first, palms facing down, and while giving the command "Fall First," crosses both arms in front of the body, palms facing down.

8. 倒地在先：场上裁判员一臂指向先倒地一方，掌心朝下，在发出"某方倒地在先"口令的同时，两臂在体前交叉，掌心朝下。

9. Simultaneous Fall: The on-field referee extends both arms straight in front of the body, palms facing down, and while giving the command "Simultaneous Fall," brings both palms downward, palms facing down.

10. Simultaneous Exit: The on-field referee bends both arms in front of the body, palms facing forward and fingertips upward, and while giving the command "Simultaneous Exit," pushes both palms forward.

11. One Side Exits: The on-field referee extends one arm towards the athlete, palm facing up, and while giving the command "One Side Exits," the other arm bends in front of the body, palm facing forward and fingertips upward, and pushes forward.

12. Designated Attack: When the referee gives the command "Both Sides Attack," both hands have the thumbs extended, with the remaining four fingers clenched into fists, palms facing down. At the same time, the arms swing inward, and the thumbs point towards each other in front of the body. If one side is designated to attack, the referee points one thumb towards the side being attacked.

13. Forced Countdown: Facing the athlete, both fists are bent in front of the body, with the palms facing forward. The fingers are gradually opened one by one, starting from the thumb, with a one-second interval.

14. Victory: The on-field referee stands between the two athletes, raises one hand while holding the wrist of the winning

9. 同时倒地：场上裁判员两臂在体前平伸，掌心向下，在发出“同时倒地”口令的同时，两掌下按，掌心朝下。

10. 同时出圈：场上裁判员两臂屈于体前，掌心朝前，指尖朝上，在发出“同 时出圈”口令的同时，两掌向前平推。

11. 一方出圈：场上裁判员一臂伸向运动员，掌心朝上，在发出“某方出圈”口令的同时，另一臂屈于体前，掌心朝前，指尖朝上，向前推出。

12. 指定进攻：场上裁判员在发出“双方进攻”口令时，两手拇指伸直，其余四指握拳，拳心朝下。同时，手臂向内摆动，两拇指在体前相对。如指定一方进攻时，则用一手拇指指向被进攻一方。

13. 强制读秒：面对运动员，两拳屈臂于体前，拳心向前，从一手拇指至小指依次张开，间隔1秒。

14. 获胜：场上裁判员站在两名运动员中间，一手握获胜运动员手腕上举。

athlete.

15. Invalid: Both arms swing crossed in front of the body, with palms facing backward.

16. Disqualification: The palms face upward, pointing towards the disqualified side, then both hands clenched into fists, and the forearms cross in front of the chest, palms facing down.

17. Warning: One arm is extended straight with the palm facing upward, pointing towards the athlete who committed the foul, and after indicating the foul, the other arm bends at a 90-degree angle, fist raised in front of the body with the fist facing backward.

18. Admonition: One arm is extended straight with the palm facing upward, pointing towards the athlete who committed the foul, and after indicating the foul, the other arm bends at a 90-degree angle, palm raised in front of the body with the palm facing backward.

19. First Aid: Facing the medical seat, both hands form an upright palm position, with the forearms crossed in front of the chest to create a cross shape.

20. One Side Steps out of the Ring: The on-field referee extends one arm towards the athlete, palm facing upward, and while giving the command "One Side Steps out of the Ring," the other arm makes an arc motion in front of the body, palm facing downward, fingertips pointing forward, and presses at the hip side.

15. 无效：两臂体前交叉摆动，掌心向后。

16. 取消资格：仰掌指向被取消资格一方，然后两手握拳，两前臂交叉于胸 前，拳心向下。

17. 警告：一臂伸直仰掌指向犯规一方运动员，在出现犯规现象后，另一臂屈 臂 90 度握拳上举于体前，拳心向后。

18. 劝告：一臂伸直仰掌指向犯规一方运动员，在出现犯规现象后，另一臂屈 臂 90 度立掌上举于体前，掌心向后。

19. 急救：面对大会医务席，两手立掌，两手臂在胸前交叉成“十”字形。

20. 一方下擂：场上裁判员一臂伸向运动员，掌心向上，在发出“某方下擂”口令的同时，另一臂与体前画弧，掌心向下，指尖向前，按于胯侧。

21. Simultaneous Step out of the Ring: The on-field referee bends both arms in front of the body, palms facing forward, and while giving the command "Simultaneous Step out of the Ring," both palms are pushed forward.

21. 同时下擂：场上裁判员两臂屈于体前，掌心朝前，指尖朝上，在发出"同时下擂"口令的同时，两掌向前平推。

第七节　太极实战推手服装与场地

Section 7: Tai Chi Push Hands Attire and Venue

Article 30: Clothing Styles and Specifications

第三十条 服装款式及规格要求

Figures 4-1: Men's Black
Figure 4-2: Men's White
Figure 4-3: Women's Black
Figure 4-4: Women's White

图 4-1：男士黑色
图 4-2：男士白色
图 4-3：女士黑色
图 4-4：女士白色

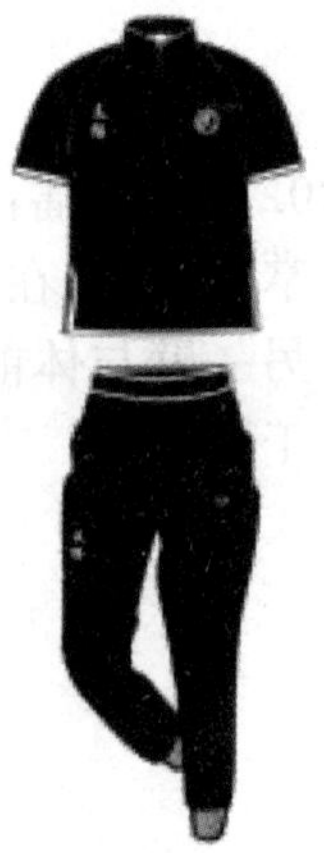

图 4–1 男士黑色

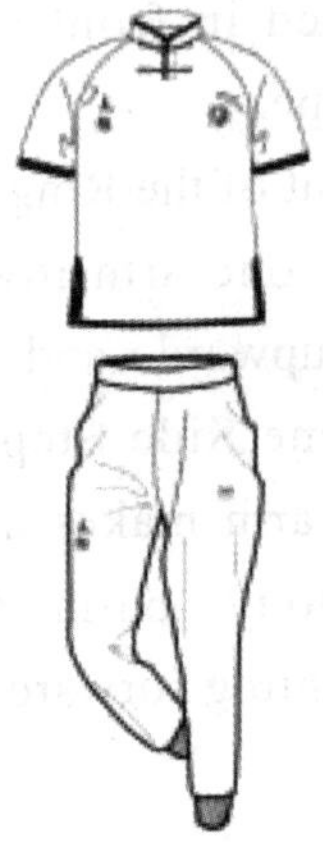

图 4–2 男士白色

图 4-3 女士黑色

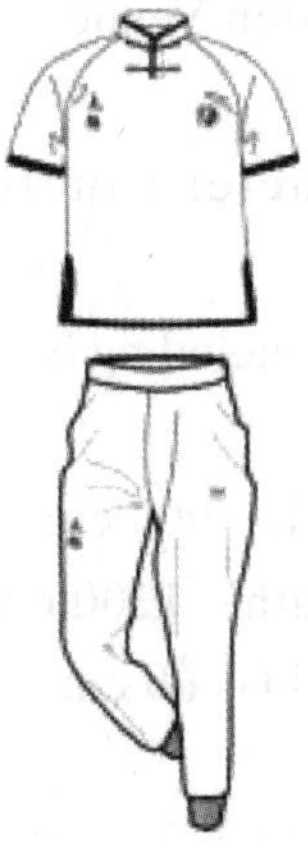

图 4-4 女士白色

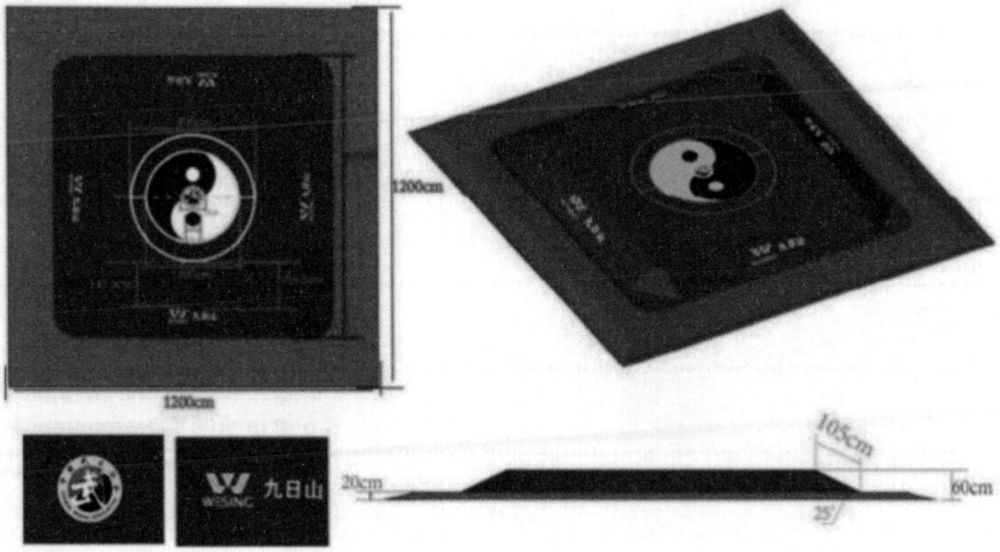

图 4-5　推手擂台

Article 31：Competition Venue	**第三十一条 比赛场地**
Center circle ciameter (including boundary lines)：60 cm	中心圈直径(含边线)：60 cm
Inner circle diameter (including boundary lines)：300 cm	内圈直径(含边线)：300 cm
Blue carpet side length：900 cm	蓝色毯面边长：900 cm
Block carpet side length：1200 cm	块毯面边长：1200 cm
Overall platform height：60 cm	整体台高：60 cm
Carpet slope：25°	毯面坡度：25°
Outer circle diameter (including boundary lines)：400 cm	外圈直径(含边线)：400 cm
Platform base height：20 cm	擂台底座高：20 cm

第五章　太极活步推手

Chapter 5: Tai Chi Moving-Step Push Hands

第一节　太极活步推手通则

Section 1: General Rules for Tai Chi Moving-Step Push Hands

第一条 竞赛项目

Article 1: Competition Events

男子太极活步推手(套路形式)对练

Men's Tai Chi Moving-Step Push Hands (Routine Form) Pair Practice

女子太极活步推手(套路形式)对练

Women's Tai Chi Moving-Step Push Hands (Routine Form) Pair Practice

混双太极活步推手(套路形式)对练

Mixed Doubles Tai Chi Moving-Step Push Hands (Routine Form) Pair Practice

第二条 确定比赛顺序

Article 2: Determination of Competition Order

在竞赛监督委员会和总裁判长的监督下,由编排记录长在技术会议后组织抽签,确 定比赛顺序。比赛如有预、决赛,决赛的比赛顺序按运动员预赛成绩由高到低确定。如 预赛排名相同,则抽签确定比赛顺序。

Under the supervision of the Competition Supervision Committee and the Chief Referee, the Chief of Arrangement and Records shall organize the draw after the technical meeting to determine the competition order. In case of preliminaries and finals, the order of the finals shall be determined based on the athletes' preliminary scores from high to low. If the preliminary rankings are the same, the competition order shall be determined by drawing lots.

Article 3: Registration

Athletes must report to the designated location 30 minutes before the competition for the first registration; the second registration shall be conducted 20 minutes before the competition; and the final registration shall be conducted 10 minutes before the competition.

Article 4: Etiquette

When athletes hear their names called for entry, complete the routine, or hear the announcement of the on-site scores, they should perform a salute to the Chief Referee. At the beginning and end of the routine, both sides of the demonstration should perform a mutual salute.

Article 5: Timing

The timing starts when the athletes start their movements from a static position and ends when they complete the entire set of movements and stand still.

第三条 检录

运动员必须在比赛前 30 分钟到达指定地点报到,参加第一次检录;赛前 20 分钟进行 第二次检录;赛前 10 分钟进行最后一次检录。

第四条 礼仪

运动员听到上场点名、完成比赛套路及现场成绩宣告时,应向裁判长行抱拳礼。套路开始与结束,演练双方互行抱拳礼。

第五条 计时

运动员由静止姿势开始动作,计时开始;当运动员完成全套动作后并步站立,计时 结束。

Article 6: Score Display

The competition results of the athletes are openly displayed.

Article 7: Forfeiture

Athletes who fail to participate in registration and the competition without valid reasons shall be considered as forfeiting, and all previously achieved results shall be invalidated.

Article 8: Doping Control

Doping control shall be conducted in accordance with the provisions of The *Olympic Charter* and the relevant requirements of the International Olympic Committee.

Article 9: Ranking

Follow the "Competition Rules and Refereeing Methods for Wushu Routines" (2012) approved by the Chinese Wushu Association and the relevant supplementary regulations.

In the doubles event, the ranking is based on the average score of the final score of each pair. The pair with the higher score takes the higher ranking.

Individual scores are ranked based on the individual scores in the doubles event. The individual with the higher score takes the higher ranking.

第六条 示分

对运动员的比赛结果公开示分。

第七条 弃权

运动员无故不参加检录与比赛，按弃权论处，之前已取得的各项成绩全部无效。

第八条 兴奋剂检测

根据《奥林匹克宪章》的规定和国际奥林匹克委员会的有关要求，进行兴奋剂检测。

第九条 名次评定

遵循中国武术协会审定的《武术套路竞赛规则与裁判法》(2012)及有关补充规定。

双人项目比赛的成绩按照每组两人成绩最后得分的平均分评定名次，双人项目得分高者名次列前。

个人成绩分别按照双人项目比赛的个人成绩评定名次，得分高者名次列前。

Handling of tied scores. In the case of tied scores, the ranking is determined in the following order:

(1) The individual with a higher level of performance is ranked higher.

(2) If there are lower invalid scores in the performance level score, the individual with the higher score excluding the lower invalid score is ranked higher.

(3) If it is still the same, the rankings are tied.

得分相同时的处理。得分相同时，按照以下顺序评定：

(1)演练水平应得分高者列前。

(2)演练水平分中的低无效分高者列前。

(3)如仍相同，名次并列。

Article 10: Routine Completion Time

第十条 套路完成时间

The time for Tai Chi Moving-Step Push Hands is 50 seconds to 1 minute.

太极活步推手时间为50秒至1分钟。

Article 11: Competition Music

第十一条 比赛音乐

Performance routines must be performed with accompanying music, which can be selected by the participants themselves.

配乐项目必须在音乐伴奏下进行，音乐自行选择。

Article 12: Competition Equipment

第十二条 比赛设备

Follow the technical standards and requirements of the Chinese University Sports Association. The venue shall comply with the standard rules.

按照中国大学生体育协会的技术标准与要求执行。场地按照规则标准执行。

第二节 太极活步推手裁判员组成及职责

Section 2: Composition and Responsibilities of Tai Chi Moving Step Push Hands Referees

Article 13: Composition of Referees

1. Main Referees

(1) Chief Referee: 1 person; Deputy Chief Referee: 1-2 persons

(2) Referee-in-Chief: 1 person; Deputy Referee-in-Chief: 1-2 persons; Referees: 3-5 persons

(3) Scheduling and Recording Chief: 1 person

(4) Check-in Supervisor: 1 person

2. Assistant Referees

(1) Scheduling and Recording Assistants: 3-5 persons

(2) Check-in Officials: 3-6 persons

(3) Announcer: 1-2 persons

(4) Sound Operator: 1-2 persons

(5) Arbitration Camera Operator: 2-4 persons

(6) Timekeeper: 1-2 persons

第十三条 裁判员组成

1. 执行裁判员

(1)总裁判长1人,副总裁判长1～2人。

(2)裁判长1人,副裁判长1～2人,裁判员3～5人。

(3)编排记录长1人。

(4)检录长1人。

2. 辅助裁判员

(1)编排记录员3～5人。

(2)检录员3～6人。

(3)宣告员1～2人。

(4)放音员1～2人。

(5)仲裁摄像员2～4人。

(6)计时员1～2人。

Article 14: Responsibilities of Referees

1. Chief Referee

(1) Organizes and leads the referee work, ensuring the implementation of competition rules and regulations, and inspecting the preparations before the competition.

(2) Interprets the rules but has no authority to modify them.

(3) Adjusts the work of the referees as needed during the competition; has the authority to handle serious referee errors.

(4) Reviews and announces the scores, and summarizes the referee work.

2. Deputy Chief Referee

(1) Assists the Chief Referee in their work.

(2) Assumes the responsibilities of the Chief Referee in their absence.

3. Referee-in-Chief

(1) Organizes referee training.

(2) Organizes and implements the referee work.

(3) Makes recommendations to the Chief Referee for appropriate action in case of serious judging errors by scoring referees.

4. Scoring Referee

(1) Obeys the leadership of the Referee, participates in referee training, and makes necessary preparations.

(2) Diligently follows the rules, independently scores, and keeps detailed records.

第十四条 裁判员职责

1. 总裁判长

(1)组织领导裁判工作，保证竞赛规则和规程的执行，检查落实赛前各项准备工作。

(2)解释规则，但无权修改规则

(3)在比赛过程中，根据比赛需要可调动裁判员工作；裁判员发生严重错误时，有权处理。

(4)审核并宣布成绩，做好裁判工作总结

2. 副总裁判长

(1)协助总裁判长工作。

(2)在总裁判长缺席时，代行其职责。

3. 裁判长

(1)组织裁判员业务学习。

(2)组织实施裁判工作。

(3)评分裁判员发生严重的评判错误时，可向总裁判长建议给予相应的处理。

4. 评分裁判员

(1)服从裁判长领导，参加裁判学习，做好准备工作。

(2)认真执行规定，独立评分，并作详细记录。

5. Scheduling and Recording Chief

(1) Organizes and arranges the arrangement and record work.

(2) Reviews registration forms and compiles the order of appearance and scorebooks according to the requirements of the conference.

(3) Prepares the necessary competition forms, reviews competition scores, and arranges rankings.

5. 编排记录长

(1)组织安排编排记录工作。

(2)审查报名表,并根据大会要求编排秩序册、成绩册。

(3)准备比赛所需的竞赛表格,审核比赛成绩及排列名次。

6. Check-In Supervisor

(1) Organizes and arranges the registration work.

(2) Conducts registration on time according to the competition order.

(3) Inspects competition attire.

(4) Organizes the registration work for award ceremonies.

6. 检录长

(1)组织安排检录工作。

(2)按比赛顺序按时检录。

(3)检查比赛服装。

(4)组织颁奖仪式的检录工作。

7. Scheduling and Recording Assistants

Carry out tasks assigned by the Scheduling and Recording Chief.

7. 编排记录员

根据编排记录长分配的任务进行工作。

8. Check-In Officials

Carry out tasks assigned by the Check-in Supervisor.

8. 检录员

根据检录长分配的任务进行工作。

9. Announcer

Introduces the competition rules, regulations, and knowledge of Wushu routines and makes timely announcements.

9. 宣告员

介绍竞赛规程、规则和武术套路运动知识,及时做好临场宣告。

10. Sound Operator

(1) Tests and plays music for the teams and makes computer backups.

(2) Plays music for the performance routines.

10. 放音员

(1)为运动队试播音乐,并做好电脑备份。

(2)为配乐项目播放配乐

11. Arbitration Camera Operator

(1) Conducts live filming of all competition events.

(2) Follows the requirements of the Arbitration Committee and Competition Supervision Committee and is responsible for playing back recorded videos of relevant events.

(3) Manages and archives all video recordings.

11. 仲裁摄像员

(1)对全部竞赛项目进行现场摄像。

(2)遵照仲裁委员会、竞赛监督委员会的要求,负责播放相关项目的录像。

(3)管理全部录像,存档保留。

12. Timekeeper

(1) Checks and verifies stopwatches before the competition.

(2) Records the routine time for each athlete in every match.

12. 计时员

(1)赛前检查核对秒表。

(2)每场比赛记录运动员套路时间。

第三节　太极活步推手仲裁委员会及其职责与申诉

Section 3: Tai Chi Moving-Step Push Hands Arbitration Committee and Its Responsibilities and Appeals

Article 15: Composition of the Arbitration Committee

The Arbitration Committee consists of a Director, Deputy Director, and Committee Members, totaling 3 or 5 individuals.

第十五条 仲裁委员会组成

由主任、副主任、委员共3人或5人组成。

Article 16: Responsibilities of the Arbitration Committee

Accept appeals from sports teams and

第十六条 仲裁委员会职责

接受运动队的申诉,并及时作出裁决,

make timely judgments, without altering the judging results.

但不改变评判结果。

Arbitration Committee members shall not participate in discussions and voting on matters related to their own affiliations.

仲裁委员会人员不参加与本人所在单位有牵连的问题的讨论与表决。

The participation of a majority of the Arbitration Committee members is required for deliberation, and decisions must be made by a majority vote. In the case of a tie vote, the Director of the Arbitration Committee has the deciding vote.

参加审议的仲裁委员会人员必须超过半数,表决时超过半数以上人员作出的决定才有效。表决投票相同时,仲裁委员会主任有决定权。

The decision of the Arbitration Committee is final.

仲裁委员会的裁决为最终裁决。

Article 17: Appeal Procedures and Requirements

第十七条 申诉程序及要求

If a sports team disagrees with the arbitration ruling, they must submit a written appeal within 15 minutes after the conclusion of the athlete's competition. The appeal must be made by the team leader or coach, accompanied by a 1000 yuan appeal fee. If the appeal is deemed valid, the appeal fee will be refunded, but the original ruling will be upheld. If the appeal is deemed invalid, the original ruling will be upheld, and the appeal fee will not be refunded, serving as a reward fund for outstanding referees.

运动队如果对裁判组的裁决结果有异议,必须在该运动员比赛结束后 15 分钟内,有本队领队或教练向仲裁委员会提出书面申诉,同时交付 1000 元申诉费。如申诉 正确,退回申诉费,但维持原判;申诉不正确的,维持原判,申诉费不退,作为优秀裁判员的奖励基金。

All teams must comply with the final decision of the Arbitration Committee. Unreasonable interference may result in serious consequences, depending on the severity, including recommendations for strict actions by the Competition Supervision Committee and the Organizing Committee.

各队必须服从仲裁委员会的最终裁决。如果无理纠缠,根据情节轻重,可以建议竞赛监督委员会、竞赛组委会给予严肃处理。

第四节 太极活步推手竞赛监督委员会及其职责

Section 4: Tai Chi Moving-Step Push Hands Competition Supervision Committee and Its Responsibilities

Article 18: Composition of the Competition Supervision Committee

第十八条 竞赛监督委员会组成

The Competition Supervision Committee consists of a Director, Deputy Director, and Committee Members, totaling 3 to 5 individuals.

由主任、副主任、委员共3 ~ 5人组成。

Article 19: Responsibilities of the Competition Supervision Committee

第十九条 竞赛监督委员会职责

Supervise and inspect the work of the Arbitration Committee.

Supervise and inspect the work of the referees.

Supervise and inspect the behavior of sports teams during the competition.

Have the authority to impose penalties for disciplinary violations by Arbitration Committee members, referees, and sports teams.

The Competition Supervision Committee does not directly participate in the responsibilities of the Arbitration Committee and the referees. It does not interfere with the proper performance of duties by the Arbitration Committee and

监督、检查仲裁委员会的工作。

监督、检查裁判员的工作。

监督、检查运动队的比赛行为。

有权对仲裁委员会人员、裁判员和运动队的违纪行为作出处罚。

竞赛监督委员会不直接参与仲裁委员会和裁判员职责范围内的工作,不干涉仲裁委 员会、裁判员正确履行自己的职责,不介入裁决结果的纠纷,不改变裁判员、仲裁委员会的裁决结果。

referees, or involve itself in disputes over the decision results or alter the decisions made by the referees or the Arbitration Committee.

第五节　太极活步推手评分方法与标准

Section 5: Scoring Methods and Standards for Tai Chi Moving-Step Push Hands

Article 20: Competition Regulations

第二十条 竞赛法则

The "Peng (warding off), Lv (rolling back), Ji (pressing), An (pushing), Cai (pulling down), Lie (splitting), Zhou (elbowing), Kao (body stroke)" elements and corresponding footwork must be used.

套路演练中应包括掤、捋、挤、按、採、挒、肘、靠八种元素。

The principles of "adhering, sticking, connecting, and following" and "combining softness and hardness" must be implemented.

套路演练中必须贯彻"粘黏连随,刚柔并济"。

Article 21: Scoring Methods and Standards for Tai Chi Push Hands

第二十一条 太极活步推手评分方法与标准

1. Scoring Methods

The maximum score for Tai Chi Push Hands competition is 10.00 points, with 5.00 points for the quality of movements and 5.00 points for the skill level of the practice.

1. 评分方法

太极活步推手比赛的满分为10.00分。其中动作质量分值为5.00分、演练水平分值为5.00分。

2. Scoring Criteria

(1) Quality of Movements

For each occurrence of other errors, deduct 0.10 to 0.3 points. Other errors include:

Holding a stationary posture for more than 2 seconds, deduct 0.1 point.

Performing non-combative practice for more than 3 seconds (non-combative meaning in the routine practice), deduct 0.1 point.

Failing to land strikes or defenses, deduct 0.1 point.

Waiting for the opponent to attack, deduct 0.1 point.

Forgetting movements, deduct 0.1 point.

Swaying (bodily movement with two-way or multi-directional displacement) or shifting (any foot or leg movement when one or both feet are supporting, causing displacement), deduct 0.1 point.

Touching the floor with the hand, deduct 0.1 point.

Dropping headwear, opening or tearing clothing, or shoes falling off, deduct 0.1 point.

Additional support (any part of the body other than the torso touching the ground due to loss of balance), deduct 0.2 points.

Falling to the ground (any part of the body other than the torso or any two other parts of the body touching the ground due to loss of balance), deduct 0.3 points.

1) If the athlete completes the routine within 5 seconds less or more than the prescribed time, deduct 0.1 point. If exceeding the prescribed time by more than

2. 评分标准

(1)动作质量

其他错误每出现一次扣0.10～0.3分。其他错误如下：

静止姿势超过2秒钟，扣0.1分。

无攻防演练超过3秒钟(套路演练过程中无技击含义超过三秒钟)扣0.1分。

击打落空或防守落空扣0.1分。

等待对方进攻扣0.1分。

遗忘扣0.1分。

晃动(躯干出现双向或多向位移)、移动(双脚或单脚或一脚一腿支撑时，任何一脚出现位移)，扣0.1分。

下撂扣0.1分。

头饰掉地，服装开纽或撕裂，鞋脱落扣0.1分。

附加支撑(由于身体失去平衡造成的，在支撑动作正常状态所需的肢体以外的身体任何一个部位(除躯干)触地)扣0.2分。

倒地(由于身体失去平衡造成的，在支撑动作正常状态所需的肢体以外，躯干或身体其他任何两个部位触地)扣0.3分。

1)运动员完成套路时间，不足或超出规定时间在5秒以内(含5秒)，扣0.1分；超出规定时间超过5秒，在10秒以内(含10秒)，扣0.2分，以此类推。

5 seconds but within 10 seconds, deduct 0.2 points, and so on.

2) When the deduction for exceeding the prescribed time reaches 0.3 points, the referee shall immediately request the athlete to stop the performance. In such cases, it is considered that the athlete did not complete the routine.

2)运动员超过规定时间扣分已达 0.3 分时,裁判长应请运动员立即收势停止比赛。此种情况应视为运动员未完成套路。

In the process of routine practice, releasing the hands no more than once and for a maximum of 5 seconds.

套路演练过程中脱手不超过一次,且时间不超过 5 秒。

(2) Skill Level

The scoring criteria for skill level are divided into three levels and nine grades based on power, coordination, rhythm, style, and music. Scores range from 5.00 to 4.21 for "good," 4.20 to 3.01 for "average," and 3.00 to 1.51 for "poor."

(2)演练水平

演练水平等级分的评分标准:按劲力、协调、节奏、风格、配乐的评分标准分为 3 档 9 级,其中 5.00 ~ 4.21 分为好、4.20 ~ 3.01 分为一般、3.00 ~ 1.51 分为不好。

档次	级别	分数段	评分标准
好	1 级	5.00 ~ 4.81	劲力充足,用力顺达,力点准确,手眼身法步及身体配合协调,节奏分明,风格突出,动作配合一致。
	2 级	4.80 ~ 4.51	
	3 级	4.50 ~ 4.21	
一般	1 级	4.20 ~ 3.81	劲力较充足,用力较顺达,力点较准确,手眼身法步及身体配合较协调,节奏分明,风格较突出,动作配合较一致。
	2 级	3.80 ~ 3.41	
	3 级	3.40 ~ 3.01	
不好	1 级	3.00 ~ 2.51	劲力不充足,用力不顺达,力点不准确,手眼身法步及身体配合不协调,节奏不分明,风格不突出,动作配合不一致。
	2 级	2.50 ~ 2.01	
	3 级	2.00 ~ 1.51	

Level	Class	Score Range	Scoring Criteria
Good Level	1	5.00 ~ 4.81	Adequate power, smooth execution of force, accurate focal points, coordinated hand-eye-body movements and body, clear rhythm, prominent style, consistent and coordinated movements
	2	4.80 ~ 4.51	
	3	4.50 ~ 4.21	
Medium Level	1	4.20 ~ 3.81	Relatively sufficient power, relatively smooth execution of force, relatively accurate focal points, relatively coordinated hand-eye-body movements and body, relatively clear rhythm, relatively prominent style, relatively consistent and coordinated movements.
	2	3.80 ~ 3.41	
	3	3.40 ~ 3.01	
Poor Level	1	3.00 ~ 2.51	Insufficient power, ineffective execution of force, inaccurate focal points, uncoordinated hand-eye-body movements and body, unclear rhythm, lack of prominent style, inconsistent and uncoordinated movements.
	2	2.50 ~ 2.01	
	3	2.00 ~ 1.51	

Article 22: Requirements for the Displayed Scores

The scores displayed by the judges and the chief judge should be rounded to two decimal places.

Article 23: Determination of Earned Score

Each judge evaluates the quality of the athlete's movements and performance level simultaneously. The average of the scores indicated by each judge represents the athlete's earned score.

第二十二条 对所示分数的要求

裁判员和裁判长所示分数到小数点后两位。

第二十三条 应得分确定

各裁判员对运动员的动作质量和演练水平同时评分。各裁判员所示分值的平均分，即为运动员的应得分。

第六节　太极活步推手服装与场地

Section 6: Tai Chi Moving-Step Push Hands Attire and Venue

Article 24: Clothing Style and Specifi-Cation Requirements

第二十四条 服装款式及规格要求

Judges should have a unified attire, and athletes must wear the competition attire specified by the Chinese Wushu Association.

裁判员统一着装,运动员必须着中国武术协会规定比赛服饰。

Article 25: Competition Venue

第二十五条 比赛场地

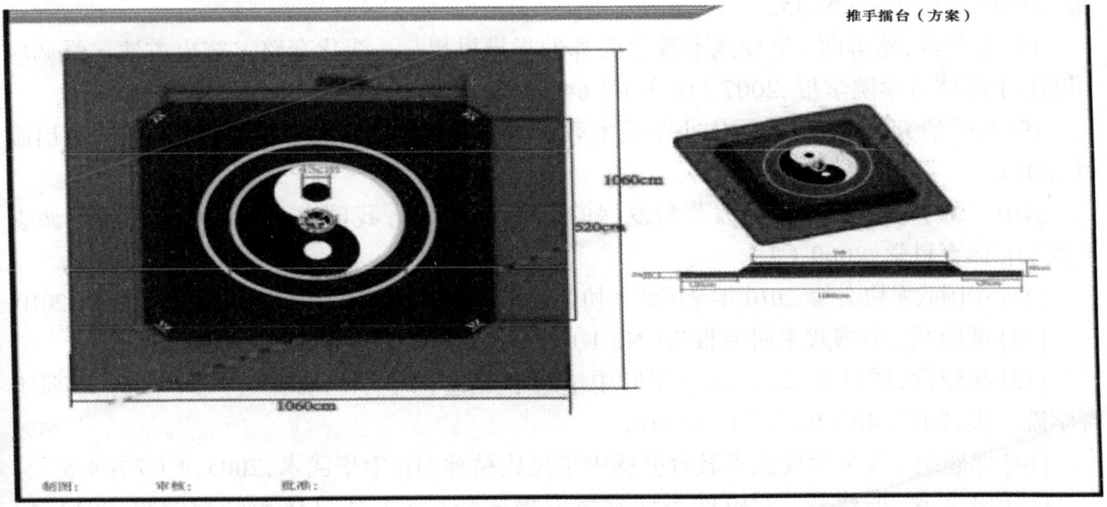

参考文献

[1] 易剑东，谢军．中国武术百年历程回顾——面向 21 世纪的中国武术 [J]. 体育文史 .1998（04）：24-26.

[2] 邱丕相，杨建营，王震．民族传统体育学科发展回顾与思考 [J]. 上海体育学院学报 .2020，44（01）：12-20.

[3] 体育院校教材编审委员会武术编选小组．体育学院本科讲义武术 [M]. 北京：人民体育出版社，1961.

[4] 教育部．教育部关于全面深化课程改革落实立德树人根本任务的意见 [Z].2014：20-22.

[5] 姜纪垒．立德树人：中国传统文化自觉的视角 [J]. 当代教育与文化，2019（01）：12-17.

[6] 中共中央办公厅国务院办公厅印发《关于实施中华优秀传统文化传承发展工程的意 见》.[EB/OL].http：//www.gov.cn/zhengce/2017-01/25/content_5163472.htm，2017-01-25 20：04.

[7] 汤立许．建国 60 年来学校武术教育发展的嬗变与走向研究 [J]. 西安体育学院学报 .2010，27（04）：449-452.

[8] 蔡仲林，施鲜丽．学校武术教学改革的指导思想——淡化套路·突出方法·强调应用 [J]. 上海体育学院学报 .2007（01）：62-64.

[9] 武术研究院组编．我国中小学武术教育改革与发展的研究 [M] 北京：高等教育出版社，2008.

[10]《关于学校武术教育改革与发展的研究》课题组．我国中小学武术教育状况调查研究 [J]. 体育科学，2009（3）.

[11] 中国武术协会编 .2010 年全国武术协会工作调研报告 [M]. 北京：中国青年出版社，2010.

[12] 戴国斌．中国武术研究报告（No.1）[M]. 北京：社会科学文献出版社，2017.

[13] 杨建营，颜世亮 .20 世纪后半叶中华武术发展中的"第一粒扣子"探寻 [J]. 成都体育学院学报，2022，48（02）：74-79+116.

[14] 课题组．改革学校武术教育弘扬中华民族精神 [J]. 中华武术，2005，4（7）：4-5.

[15] 田金龙，杨建营．太极推手课堂教学模式新探 [J]. 武汉体育学院学报，2013，47（08）：77-81.

[16] 范江涛，武冬．太极拳概念的论定 [J]. 邯郸学院学报，2022，32（04）：28-41.

[17]（清）王宗岳等著，沈寿点校．太极拳谱 [M]. 第二版．北京：人民体育出版社，2006.

[18] 季培刚 . 太极往事 - 晚清以来太极拳的传承系谱 [M]. 北京：中国商业出版社，2011.

[19] 刘靖 . 太极拳现代教学改革研究 [J]. 南京体育学院学报(自然科学版),2013,12(06)：139-141.

[20] 刘智宇 . 太极拳课程教学优化对高中女生身心健康的促进研究 [D]. 上海体育学院，2022；59.

[21] 付雯 . 对普通高校太极拳技击教学改革的探索 [J]. 首都体育学院学报,2005(02)：99-100.

[22] 田金龙,杨建营 . 太极推手课堂教学模式新探 [J]. 武汉体育学院学报,2013,47(08)：77-81.

[23] 杨建营,王家宏 . 三种武术教育改革思想辨析 [J]. 武汉体育学院学报,2015,49(08)：5-12.

[24] 赵光圣,戴国斌 . 我国学校武术教育现实困境与改革路径选择——写在“全国学校体育武术项目联盟”成立之际 [J]. 上海体育学院学报,2014,38(01)：84-88.

[25] 田金龙,钱源泽,肖维加等 . 太极推手技法研究 [J]. 中华武术,2020,No.435(10)：71-75.

[26] 顾留馨,沈家桢 . 陈式太极拳 [M]. 北京：人民体育出版社,2013.3.

[27] (明)戚继光著；盛冬铃点校 . 纪效新书 [M]. 北京：中华书局,1996.

[28] 杨澄甫 . 太极拳使用法 [M]. 上海文光印书馆,民国二十年(1931).

[29] 刘晚苍,刘石樵著 . 太极拳架与推手 [M]. 上海：上海教育出版社,1980.

[30] 董斌传授；王玫瑰,王明波整理 . 太极拳心法传真 [M]. 上海：上海大学出版社,2017.

[31] 郭福厚 . 太极拳秘诀评解 [M]. 天津：天津科学技术出版社,1993.

[32] 田金龙,邱丕相 . 太极拳技术原型的提炼与推手技术体系的构建 [J]. 上海体育学院学报,2013,37(06)：77-80.

[33] 吴文瀚,武派太极拳体用全书 [M]. 北京：北京体育大学出版社,2001.

[34] 徐亚奎,杨建营 . 太极拳技击实战比赛的进阶模式设计 [J]. 体育科学,2022,42(12)：68-76+85.

[35] 张文鼎编著 . 老子太极拳本原 [M]. 武汉：湖北科学技术出版社,2017.

[36] 吴耀科 . 拳论摘要 [Z].

[37] 宋书铭 . 太极功(抄本)[Z].

[38] 吴鉴泉 . 吴式家传太极拳体用全书——太极法说(抄本)[Z].

[39] 郝为真 . 王宗岳太极拳论 [Z].

[40] 季培刚 . 太极往事 - 晚清以来太极拳的传承系谱 [M]. 北京：中国商业出版社,2001.

[41] 陈鑫 . 陈氏太极拳图说 [M]. 太原：山西科学技术出版社,2006.

[42] 孙禄堂 . 孙禄堂武学集注 [M]. 北京：北京科学技术出版社,2018.

[43] 于志均 . 太极拳理论解读 [M]. 北京：中国人民大学出版社,2012.

[44] 中国大学生体育协会 . 中国大学生太极推手锦标赛竞赛规则 [Z].2019,01.

[45] 国家体委 . 武术太极推手竞赛规则 [M]. 北京：人民体育出版社,1994.